HOPE
FROM THE
Garden of Eden
TO THE END OF THE
PATMOS ISLAND

HOPE
FROM THE
Garden of Eden
TO THE END OF THE
PATMOS ISLAND

ANDREW CHOI

Copyright © 2021 by Andrew Choi.

All rights reserved. No part of this publication may be reproduced, distributed, or transmitted in any form or by any means, including photocopying, recording, or other electronic or mechanical methods, without the prior written permission of the author, except in the case of brief quotations embodied in critical reviews and certain other noncommercial uses permitted by copyright law.

This is a work of fiction. Names, characters, business, events and incidents are the products of the author's imagination. Any resemblance to actual persons, living or dead, or actual events is purely coincidental.

Printed in the United States of America
ISBN 978-1-64133-902-5 (hc)
ISBN 978-1-64133-903-2 (sc)
ISBN 978-1-64133-904-9 (e)

Library of Congress Control Number: 2021920768

Religion/Self-Help
10.08.2021

MainSpring Books
5901 W. Century Blvd
Suite 750
Los Angeles, CA, US, 90045

www.mainspringbooks.com

Table of Contents

Chapter 1 Redemption And The Restoration:
           Hope Message From The Beginning 1

    God's Creation of the Happy Life 3
    The Promise of the Coming Messiah at the time of Fall 10
    God's unchangeable promise of love showed
        in the beautiful rainbow 22
    Recognizing the Lord's Guidance in time of difficulty:
        Discerning God's Direction 26
    The Bright Morning of Jacob Jacob changed as a new person, Israel . 32

Chapter 2 Jesus Christ, Messiah, Gives Hope Message 39

    The Awesome concept that God brought at Christmas 40
    The Law and Grace 45
    Christ will give you eternal life 51
    The Song of Victory on Passion day 59
    Christ's Cross as the Hope of Humankind 62
    Victory over the power of death as He resurrected 71
    Reconciliation with God and the Restoration of the True Eden:
        Four Spiritual Principles 76

Chapter 3 Hope On The Days Of Trials 83

    Look up to God, who gives you a Positive Perspective and Hope 84
    Look up to God, Who Disciplines and Refines You Like
        Gold in Times of Suffering 93
    Look up to Jesus When Strong Storms Blow into Your Life 99
    Be hopeful and Focus on the future goal 105
    Commit Thy Way To The Lord 108
    Ebenezer: Thus Far the Lord has helped Us 113

Chapter 4	Compassionate Love Of God And His Forgiveness Give Hope	117

Truthful Love 118
God's Unconditional Love Completes Our Lives 122
Forgive As the Father Forgives You 127
The Joy of Finding the Lost..133

Chapter 5	Hope Of The 21st Century: Messianic Message Of The New Hope And The Justice Of The World	139

Relevant Personal History of the Author 148

Chapter 6	The Power Of God That Strengthens You	155

God's Power Makes It Possible for the People of Israel to
  Cross the Red Sea 156
God's Almighty Power Makes Miracles Still Possible 166
God's Power Lifted up Elijah When He Was Depressed 172
One Changed person changed the World......................................178

Chapter 7	Hopeful Life	187

If You have Hope, Wait Patiently 188
Living Faith, Living Hope..194
I Will Glorify You 201
The Highway to Heaven Is Wide Open..209
Christ's Coming Back: Hope for the Generations 218

BIBLIOGRAPHY...227

CHAPTER 1

REDEMPTION AND THE RESTORATION: HOPE MESSAGE FROM THE BEGINNING

God's Creation of the Happy Life
Genesis Chapters 1-2

THESE TWO CHAPTERS OF GENESIS, WHICH are the accounts of creation and the Garden of Eden, cover the broad spectrum of the origin of human beings, the beginning of the universe, and the first humans' assimilation into life in the Garden of Eden. The phrase "in the beginning" and the verb "created" in Genesis 1:1 share the same word root that means continuing creation. In the Hebrew language, the noun *beginning* describes not just existing things but also moving objects. So, although *beginning* is the noun, it tells about God the Father and the Son of God creating the universe and continuing to do the work of creation that sustains the universe. The concept of Christ as the Creator with God the Father echoes the first verse of Genesis and the gospel of John: "In the beginning God created the heavens and the earth" (Genesis 1:1 KJV). "In the beginning was the Word, and the Word was with God. The same was in the beginning with God. All things were made by him; and without him was not anything made that was made" (John 1:1–3 KJV).

These two chapters of the Bible concern themselves with the principles of a perfect, happy life. We all anticipate happy lives. Everyone has a map of happiness, and they pursue this plan in their own ways. However, there are specific precepts and an accurate map to follow to reach that land. These two chapters in our Bible today are a fine road map for all of us to reach a happy life. With these two chapters, I would like to focus on the subject of God loving the world and creating perfect happiness for humans. The Garden of Eden is the original palace where humans should be placed, but humans lost that palace. Someone would have to win back that land. John Milton wrote two important books concerning this topic. One book is entitled *Paradise Lost*, the other book is entitled *Paradise Restored*.

These two chapters of Genesis speak about the paradise that was lost, and this picture gives us the concept of the kingdom that Christ promised to us, which would be a paradise restored.

Eden means "delightfulness." So the Garden of Eden means the garden of delightfulness. In Genesis, God has basically two names: the first is Elohim, which means almighty; the second name is Jehovah, which means the God of love. In the first chapter when God created the heavens and the earth, God's name is referred to as Elohim. So, Genesis 1:1 can be read as, "In the beginning the almighty God created the heaven and the earth." Then, in Genesis 2:4, God is referred as Jehovah God, so it can be read as, "When the God of love made the earth and heavens, He created the garden of happiness." When God created the Garden of Eden, God planned for the perfect happy garden. His love, mighty power, and wisdom made it possible.

Just like good parents want to give the best lives to their children and prepare them for happy lives, the Lord, Jehovah, who is our heavenly parent, wished for our best and made every condition possible for the achievement of human happiness in the Garden of Eden. He also had the ability to make the garden perfectly. So, in the Garden of Eden, we can find the glorious condition of happiness. Before we learn about the conditions of perfect happiness that existed in the Garden of Eden, let me ask you a question. What do you do for your happiness? What is happiness? What do you need for a happy life? What conditions are you missing now for that happiness?

If you find your shortcomings, pray to God that He would fill you with blessings. God, who is almighty (Elohim) and loving (Jehovah), will provide those blessings for you.

Here are some conditions that are necessary to have a happy life.

First are basic survival needs. For example, the basic human needs for survival in the desert are one cot, a warm heater, water, and food.

The next requirements for human basic needs are safety and security, which are expansions of the basic needs. We are referring to constant stability, not just temporary satisfaction. Examples of constant stability would be job security and family security. Safety and security also include freedom from fear, freedom from anxiety and chaos, and the need for safe boundaries.

Third, we need life goals that would be meaningful and pleasant for life. This meaningful goal of life rises to the next level of safety. When people sense safety and security, and when their emotions are stabilized, they will be capable of establishing and accomplishing goals in their daily lives.

Fourth, we need love and belonging. These are important issues not just for teenagers but for everyone in their stages of life. All human beings need community, family, and friends: where they can belong, where they can be appreciated, and where they can love and be loved.

The fifth human need is self-esteem. People need to be respected by others. The sixth human need is self-actualization. This is when people are able to reach their peak performance, independent of primitive needs. More fully functioning and creative people can achieve their dreams, yet not many people are at this stage.

One of my elders from my previous church, who was about sixty years old, told me that he had many dreams in his life. However, he never achieved even one dream. He once wanted to become a writer; then he wanted to be a musician and a pastor. He also wanted to be a good father. Another time, he wanted to be a rich millionaire. He said, "I never achieved any of those dreams, and I gave up each one of those dreams. Now I only need to be satisfied with my life just as it is."

We all have needs and wants, whether we come from simple beginnings or from the highest ranks of society. Some of us may never be satisfied in this world no matter what state we find ourselves. We all strive to be better and go further to find satisfaction and happiness. But what is the real condition of happiness? What do we need for happiness?

Let us look at the Garden of Eden to find the conditions of happiness.

First, the basic physical needs were met in the Garden of Eden. Christianity primarily focuses on spirituality, but Christianity does not depart from material things (as many believe). Christianity does not ignore the basic needs of humans. In fact, there is a misunderstanding in the Christian religion whereby certain people feel that Christianity despises material wealth. God never intended for us to suffer in poverty. In special circumstances of God's providence (and to serve the suffering Lord), we sometimes can choose to content ourselves with the situation of poverty. However, God is not condemning material things. In fact, as you see here in the days of creation, God carefully designed a world that could produce abundant foods, beautiful trees, and a comfortable environment. Allow me to share a few verses in Genesis 1:28–29 (KJV): "And God blessed them, and God said unto them, Be fruitful, and multiply, and replenish the earth, and subdue it and have dominion over the fish of the sea, and over the fowl of the air, and over every living thing that moveth upon the earth. And God said, Behold, I have given you every hear bearing seed, which is upon the face of all the earth, and every tree, in which is the fruit of tree yielding seed; to you it shall be meat." In chapter 2, verses 8 and 9 (KJV) say, "And the Lord God planted a garden eastward in Eden; and there he put the man whom he had formed. And out of the ground made the Lord God to grow every tree that is pleasant to the sight, and good for food; the tree of life also in the midst of the garden, and the tree of knowledge of good and evil." As you can see here, God gave us a rich environment in the Garden of Eden.

The Garden of Eden also had rich rivers. There were four rivers that ran through the Garden of Eden. The first river was named Pishon. It encircled the land of Havilah, probably a district in Eastern Arabia, which was a land of gold and precious stones. In modern times this river could be the Indus or the Ganges, or perhaps it was the ocean around Arabia. The second river was named Gihon. It encircled Ethiopia. Traditionally, people believe that this river was the Nile. The third river was the Hiddekel. It flows east of Assyria, literally in front of Assyria. The fourth river has the Hebrew name Prah, and it means Euphrates—the greatest river in the world. The location of the Garden of Eden was around the Tigris and Euphrates, and it is surmised that the Garden of Eden was in the vicinity around Armenia. A river symbolizes abundance, a rich culture, and prosperity. Every city that is located around the river prospers, and the culture blossoms. So, in the Garden of Eden, God not only meets our basic needs but gives us the optimal capability for abundance. The third condition of the Garden of Eden was a pleasant job and goals to achieve. The Garden of Eden is not a garden where we do not have to do anything, but it is a pleasant place to work. Therefore, to have a happy life, you need a pleasant job. Retirement would be good for relaxing for a little while. But if there is nothing to do, it would be a nightmare, not a heaven. We always need some constructive things to do and we have pleasant job to do at the Garden of Eden. When the Lord God made the earth and heaven- there were no shrub of the field. No plants of the field had yet sprung up. It was uncultured desert. Why? Because there was no man to work on the ground, it was a desolate place. Streams came up from the earth and watered the whole surface of the ground. The Lord made human beings so that they could cultivate the Garden of Eden. Every law material was provided sufficiently, but still there were many things to do to make their land as a delightful land. So, there were challenges and goals to achieve. If it is not overwhelming, the challenge is good for the healthy life and it is the condition of a happy life.

The fourth condition of happiness is love and belonging. What was the first institution that God created? It was the family. In the Garden of Eden there was one beautiful family—the family of Adam and Eve. The Lord God viewed Adam and found that he needed company—a helper with whom he could belong. The Lord caused the man to fall into a deep sleep. While he was sleeping, He took one of the man's ribs and closed up the place with flesh. Then God made a woman from the rib He had taken out of the man, and He brought her to the man. The man said, "This is now bone of my bones and flesh of my flesh." This was the first couple, which ultimately became the ancestors of all human beings.

God's first created institution was the family because human beings need to be loved and they need to live in a group where they could have a sense of belonging. This dynamic is essential to a happy life. Even if someone had every material thing in the world, if there is no one who loves him or her, life would be miserable. Those who have a strong character have a favorite word, "God alone is my fortress." That is an important factor in faith. However, strong faith is not enough for our happiness. Although you have faith in God, you still need others whom you can love and whom you can lean on them. I do not think that any human beings can be independent from others. Children, who reach a certain age, want to be independent from their parents. That is very natural for the young adult to establish his/her own personal identity. But there is not total independence in any human relationship. More importantly, the happiness comes when they find someone whom they can belong. Jay Keesler, former president of Taylor University said, "One of my great hope in life is wind up with at least eight people who will attend my funeral without once checking their watches" Who could be those people? I believe it would be the family that we could belong to each other's.

We can find that the fifth condition of a happy life as we find the positive self-esteem. Positive self-esteem comes when we find God's Image in us. In Genesis 1:24-28, it says, "And God said, Let the earth bring forth the living creature after his kind, cattle, and creeping thing, and beast of the earth after his kind: and it was so. And God made the beast of the earth cattle after their kind, and everything that creepeth upon the earth after his kind, and God saw that it was good. And God said, Let us make man in our image, after our likeness: and let them dominion over the fish of the sea, and the fowl of the air, over the cattle, and over the earth, and over every creeping thing creepth upon the earth. So, God created man in his own image, man in the image of God created he him; male and female he created he them." (Genesis 2:24-27, KJV) When we look at ourselves as God's creature that was made by God's image, we will restore the dignity in our self-image. It is so important to look at ourselves as God views us, because it changes our perspective on life. If we look at ourselves according to a materialistic view, we are no better than other material things, mammals'. Psalmist, with his amazement for the awesomeness of God's creation of in-most beings of human sang, "For thou hast possessed my reins: thou hast covered me in my mother's womb. I will praise thee; for I am fearfully and wonderfully made: marvelous are thy works; and that my soul knoweth right well. My substance was not hid from thee, when I was made in secret, and curiously wrought in the lowest parts of the earth. Thine eyes did see my substance, yet being unperfect; and in thy book all my members were written, which in continuance were fashioned, when as yet there was none of them!" (Psalms 139: 13-16, KJV)

God gave us the treasures of God in our heart and minds; that is the image of God, therefore, we should not be bounded by a negative and demeaning self-portrait. We should be free from that negativity. You may not have found your strength yet. But God has created every human being according to His image. God's dignity, His holiness and His essence of love remain within you!

Salvation means that we are getting the restored image of God in ourselves as we imitate Christ. Our life and image could reflect, resemble Christ.

Additionally, we can find that the fifth condition of a happy life is spiritual life in the Garden of Eden. God made human as a spiritual being. God formed the human from dust and gave His Spirit by giving breath through the nostril. At that moment, human became a living being. Thus, without spiritual life, there would be no contentment, happiness, and satisfaction in human life. Without spiritual life, human is no more living being, but the dust of the ground.

The last and most important condition of a delightful garden was life that lasts forever. In the Garden of Eden, there was no death. What were the two important trees in the middle of garden? One was the tree of knowledge of good and evil. Another was the tree of life. The tree of life was the tree that produces the fruit that enables human to live forever. Satan took away this privilege of "Eternal life" that God originally allowed in the Garden of Eden. That was the fatal and final damage to the happiness of human beings. Long and healthy life is considered as an important condition of blessedness in every culture and every nation. Everlasting life is not just long life; it is a life that has free communion with the living God. Everlasting life was guaranteed in the Garden of Eden. We could live in a land free from the dear of death, free from the pain of sorrow. Unfortunately, we could not keep this privilege. Yet in Jesus Christ, God restored our ultimate condition of happiness, which is the eternal life. Our Lord promised us, "Jesus said unto her, I am the resurrection, and the life: he that believed in me, though he were dead, yet shall he live." (John 11:25, KJV)

God so love the world and he created the perfect happy garden in the land of Eden in the beginning. Since our heavenly Father is a good Father, He wants to give us perfect happy life. Our happiness is important to Him. Although we live in a lost paradise, we still pursue happiness, which is hard to find. However, since Christ can restore and enable us to enter the kingdom of God, He can restore our true happiness.

The Promise of the Coming Messiah at the time of Fall
Genesis 3:1–19

At the moment when humans fell, God had already given the promise of restoration and provided the remedy. That remedy was Jesus Christ. Humans fell, but God did not fail in executing His redemptive plan. Evil bruises us, but God gives us restoration and victory through our Lord and Savior. Therefore, Jesus is our hope beyond the conflicts, bitterness, divisions, and disasters in this world.

Absolute goodness and perfect happiness

Genesis chapters 1 and 2 could be titled "The Age of Innocence." In this age of innocence, God gave a perfectly happy world to Adam and Eve. Innocence sometimes looks like ignorance, and there was a common ground connecting the world's innocence with Adam and Eve's ignorance.

Innocence: When human beings are not exposed to the temptation of sin, they are innocent.

Ignorance: When human beings have never experienced evil, they are ignorant of what evil and good are.

I call this state of ignorance that comes from innocence the "absolute goodness," because there is not even a concept of evil.

In one of the Disneyland movie, "Alice' Adventure in Wonderland" by *Lewis Carroll*, we can see naïve person as a person who has no concept of evil at all. In that movie, Alice's naivetés, who almost looks ignorant, could explain that she has no concept of evil. When Alice falls down a rabbit hole, naïve girl, Alice is downright ignorant. At the end, Alice matures into self-sufficient girl.[1] There also was a drama called "Welcome to Dong Mack Gol

---

[1] https://www.quora.com/Storytelling-Who-are-the-best-inquenus-characters-in-literature-film-and-television

Village"[2] that took place when the Korean peninsula was going through the horrible war between its two parts, North Korea and South Korea. In a deep mountain, there was a village called Dong Mack Gol, whose people were so naive that they did not know about anything that was happening outside of their village. They lived so peacefully because they did not even know there was a war. You could call them ignorant, yet they were innocent people. They really had happy lives because of that.

In the garden of Eden, Adam and Eve had eternal life, happiness, peace, abundance, beauty, and the joy of achievement that comes with doing one's job; they had all of this because they did not know anything about evil or sin.

Why was there perfect and absolute happiness? Because there was 100 percent complete trust between God and human beings. Why did God forbid them the fruit from the Tree of Knowledge of Good and Evil?

God wanted to keep human beings in their innocence because He blessed the human being to have a privilege to live in the garden of Eden, where there was only absolute goodness. That was why God forbid eating the fruit from the tree of knowledge of good and evil. Adam and Eve never need to be exposed to evil to know what is good. Knowing the difference between good and evil could result in experiencing evil in some way. God did not want those negative things to befall human beings. Eve did not understand why God forbade eating from this tree. As the Tempter deceived her and said, 'For God knows that when you eat of it your eyes will be opened, and you will be like God, knowing good and evil', she disobeyed God and invited Adam to participate in eating from the tree of knowledge of good and evil.

That was the fall of human being and start of the misery of human-kinds.

Genesis chapter 3 describes the Human beings fall. This chapter recounts the reality of the human condition after the fall. Chapter 3:1–19 could be called "The Age of Darkness." As the consequence of sin, human species experienced alienation from God, a sense of loss, irresponsibility, and loneliness; most of all, they experienced spiritual and physical death. In the Eden post-fall, death is not just separation from life. It is the complete separation from God's redemptive love. God said to Adam, "For dust you are and to dust you will return."

---

[2] Welcome to Dongmakgol (웰컴 투 동막골) korean film 2005, www.koreanmovie.com/ Welcome_to_Dongmakgol_km491/ (accessed on 18 August, 2011).

It is a very dark picture.

As we read about God's punishment of Adam and Eve at Genesis chapter 3: 14-19, it seems that the human species was done and that God was not going to give them any more chances. God seems to be saying, "You are done! I will not see you anymore!"

However, the focus in Genesis 3 is not on the problems, but on the remedy. The focus here is not on the conditions, but on God's plan to restore paradise and redemption. Therefore, there is hope in the midst of misery.

In this chapter, we can see the hope beyond failure; it is the hope beyond suffering. It is the hope beyond temptation, failure, and conflicts; it is the hope beyond guilt. Verse 15, which foreshadows the beginning of the gospel, can be called "the primitive" gospel. Although there are many problems in the world, we will not dwell on problems and misery. Instead, we will focus on hope, because God had a redemptive plan at the moment of fall—and still does.

The Dark Reality of Satan's Evilness

To find the light in the midst of the darkness, we need to first admit the reality of the darkness. When we dare to look through the darkness, we can find the light at the end of the long, dark tunnel

In his book, *Your Adversary the Devil*, Dwight Pentecost compares the tactics of a physical battle to those of a spiritual one. He states that, "No military commander can expect to be victorious in battle unless he understood his enemy. Should he prepare for an attack by the land, ignored the possibility that the enemy might approach by air or by sea, he would open the way to defeat. Or should he prepare for a land and sea attack and ignore the possibility of an attack through the air, he would certainly jeopardize the campaign."[3]

In our daily struggle with Satan, we cannot be victorious unless we understand our Enemy's tactics and plans. Within our beliefs, we encourage positive optimism. However, our beliefs should not mislead us into unrealistically naïve; not get in touch with the reality or just ignoring the

---

[3] J. Dwight Pentecost, Your Adversary The Devil, (Grand Rapids, MI: Kregel Publication, 1969), Introduction.

painful fact of life. We have to clearly see the cold reality as well. Genesis 3 helps us look at the real world more objectively, which reveals the spiritual and physical conditions of life after the fall. We must admit the reality of Satan and evil forces in this world. As Dwight said, people cannot have victory unless they understand their adversary's philosophy, methods of operation, and methods of temptation. If we blindly deny the fact of the Enemy's existence, or if we choose to escape instead of fighting with him, we are just hiding from reality. Consequently, we would ultimately be defeated. There is a saying in Asian classical battle principle by Sun Tzu (c. 6th century BC) who was a Chinese General, military strategist, and author of The Art of War, an immensely influential ancient Chinese book on military strategy; said,." Know your enemy and know yourself, find naught in fear for 100 battles. Know yourself but not your enemy, find level of loss and victory. Know thy enemy but not yourself, wallow in defeat every time." (知彼知己, 百戰不殆)[4]

So who is Satan? Satan is described as "the serpent, which is craftier than any of the wild animals the Lord God had made" (Genesis 3:1). This verse tells us a few things about Satan.

First, Satan is a creature who is under God's control.

Satan is like other creatures, a being that God has made. Since every creature is under God's control, Satan is too. When trials last a long time, we are afraid that the Enemy will destroy us. However, Satan's attack is limited because our good Lord controls evil. In the book of Job, there is an interesting story about Satan.

Job 1:6–11 says,

"Now there was a day when the sons of God came to present themselves before the Lord, and Satan came also among them. And the Lord said unto Satan, Whence comest thou? Then Satan answered the Lord, and said, From going to and fro in the earth, and from walking up and down in it. And the Lord said unto Satan, Hast thou considered my servant Job, that three is none like him in the earth, a perfect and an upright man, one that feareth God, and escheweth evil? Then Satan answered the Lord, and said, Doth Job fear God for naught? Hast not thou made an hedge about him, and about

---

4   Sun Tzu, The Art of War, (6th century BC) Ch. 3, From Wikiquote, http://en.wikiquote.org/ wiki/Sun_Tzu (accessed on August 25, 2011).

his house, and about all that he hath on every side? Thou hast blessed the work of his hands, and his substance is increased in the land. But put forth thine hand now, and touch all that he hath, and he will curse thee to thy face." (Job 1:6-11, KJV)

Here, we can see that Satan is the one who accuses, promotes temptation and destruction. By doing so, Satan put adversary to human beings. In fact, the word Satan literally means "adversary" The job of Satan and his fallen angels is to put people adversary before God and to put individuals against God.

Satan is personal and supernatural. However, we should not give God's attributes and power to Satan, because Satan is a creature of God. Satan does his work only by God's permission. Theologically, Satan is controlled. Therefore, God limits evil's plan and actions. Whenever misery and chaos appear in the world, at some point the destruction stops and a catharsis occurs. In other words, at some point God steps in and limits the destruction Satan perpetrates. If the Almighty did not curb Satan's destruction, human beings would continue on the downward spiral of chaos.

Nonetheless, Satan and his fallen angels have become the spiritual force of evil in the world. Names of Satan are the Devil, the Tempter, the Evil One, the Accuser, the Enemy, the prince of demons, the ruler of this world, and the prince of the power of the air (Ephesians 6:10–12).

Second, verse 1 says, "The serpent was the craftiest creature of all that God had made," which indicates that this creature has the ability to tempt and deceive. Therefore, Satan is the Tempter.

Let us observe and learn the nature and tactics of the Enemy. Here are some facts about the Tempter: Satan asked Eve, "Did God really say, 'You must not eat from any tree in the garden?'" Satan asked a question to Eve that could cause her to doubt about the truthfulness of God's word and his love. It was like a sharp sword with the poison thrown into the heart of Eve. Satan at the onset twisted the word of God and emphasized that God was restricting them and hiding something good for them. Eve replied, "" (Genesis 3:2–3).

Satan did not, however, emphasize God's abundant grace and provision when He said, "You may eat any fruit from the trees in the garden, except one."

You see, God allowed humans to eat all the fruits in the garden. More importantly, God gave Adam and Eve the Tree of Life. This was a great provision for the creature who was made from dust. However, Eve forgot all of that goodness from God and just concentrated on the fact that God forbade them to eat the Tree of Knowledge of Good and Evil.

When we are not focusing on the grace of God or being grateful, instead in a mood of complaining and focusing on the negativity, Satan is already beginning to occupy our minds. Be aware of this.

What happened when Satan questioned the human being about God's word, and the human being doubted the love of God?

The trust relationship between God and human beings had been broken. Human beings had to run away from God and hide themselves from Him. To the hiding humans, God asked, "Where are you?" Adam and Eve were hiding from God because they doubted the love of God and felt guilty.

In a contrast, when the Tempter questioned Jesus about God's love, Christ replied, "Do not put the Lord your God to the test." Trusting each other is the most important essence in every human relationship. If one person starts to question the integrity of others and if that person continues to focus on doubts, especially in the relationship between spouses, that person will damage the love relationship. Sooner or later, the union will break. This exact broken relationship happened when the human being doubted God's love.

Third, Satan is an expert of stimulation for evil purposes and promotes empty and proud dreams.

Satan stimulated Eve's pride and ambition by saying, "You will be like God." She was then tempted. Jesus, in comparison to Eve, humbled Himself and obeyed until He died on the cross. Socrates reminds us to know ourselves. We are mere creatures who were made from dust. Therefore, we should not look for any vainglory. Humbleness starts from knowing that we come from dust. This wisdom would enable us to move away from the temptation of Satan.

Fourth, Satan is an expert on the tactics that promote greediness.

After Eve was influenced by Satan's temptation, she looked at the tree. The fruit of the Tree of Good and Evil looked so good and desirable.

Human beings are neither angels nor demons

What is the nature of human beings in general? A human being is a tension-filled entity capable of various possibilities, divine and demonic. So, as one Asian proverb says, we are not responsible for our faces when we are born because God makes us as we are. However, we are responsible for our faces as we get older. Does your face reflect the divine or tend to resemble the demonic? Humans have both possibilities. We have free will. That means we have ability either chooses to follow God' will or cooperate with Satan. If we are willing to choose the divine will, we will be able not to yield to sin. However, if we choose to follow evil we can do so as well.

I want to share the story of how *Leonardo da Vinci* completes the picture of *The Last Supper*.

"Leonardo da Vinci took seven years to complete *The Last Supper*. The figures representing the twelve apostles and Christ were painted from living persons. He chose the life model for the painting of the figure of Jesus first. When it was decided that da Vinci would paint this great picture, hundreds of young men were carefully viewed in an endeavor to find a face and personality exhibiting innocence and beauty, free from the scars and signs of dissipation caused by sin. Finally, after weeks of laborious searching, he selected a young man of nineteen as a model for the portrayal of Christ. For six months, da Vinci worked on his depiction of this leading character in his famous painting. During the next six years, da Vinci continued his labors on this sublime work of art. One by one, fitting persons were chosen to represent each of the eleven apostles, space being left for the final task: the painting of the figure representing Judas Iscariot. Judas was the apostle who betrayed his Lord for thirty pieces of silver, worth about seventeen dollars in our present day currency. For weeks, da Vinci searched for a man with a hard, callous face, with a countenance marked by scars of avarice, deceit, hypocrisy, and crime; a face that would delineate a character who would betray his best friend.

After many discouraging experiences searching for the person to represent Judas, word came to da Vinci that a man whose appearance fully met his requirements had been found. The candidate was in a Roman prison, sentenced to die for a life of crime and murder. da Vinci made the trip to Rome at once. The man was brought out from his dungeon cell and led into the light of the sun. There Da Vinci saw before him a dark, swarthy man with long, unkempt hair. His face portrayed a character of viciousness and complete ruin. At last, the famous artist had found the subject needed to represent the character of Judas in his painting.

By special permission from the king, this prisoner was taken to Milan, where the picture was being painted. For months he sat before da Vinci at appointed hours each day as the gifted artist diligently continued his task of transmitting to his canvas this base character representing the traitor and betrayer of our Savior. As he finished his last stroke, he turned to the guards and said, "I have finished. You may take the prisoner away." As the guards were leading their prisoner away, he suddenly broke loose from their control and rushed up to da Vinci, crying as he did so, "Oh, da Vinci, look at me! Do you not know who I am?" With eyes trained to note detail, da Vinci carefully scrutinized the man upon whose face he had constantly gazed for six months and replied, "No, I have never seen you until you were brought before me out of the dungeon in Rome." Then, lifting his eyes toward heaven, the prisoner exclaimed, "Oh, God, have I fallen so low?" Then, turning his face to da Vinci, he cried, "Look at me again, because I am the same man you painted seven years ago as the figure of Christ."

Leonardo da Vinci was shocked that the person he drew as demonic was the same person he had drawn as angelic a long time ago."[5]

---

[5] "The Pathos Behind Da Vinci's-Last Supper", Articles on Revelation File News

Therefore, human beings are neither angels nor demons. Human beings are in between and possess both possibilities. Tension exists because of this.

Unfortunately, the first human being chose to listen to the Tempter. As the consequence of disobeying God's word and choosing the Tempter's advice, human beings started to experience alienation from God, broken relationships, loneliness, shame, guilty consciences, and the bondage of sin and death. The most miserable thing is the fact that death came to all people as the consequence of the first human beings disobeying God's word. Death means not just the physical death but the separation from God's redemptive love and from life.

At the judgment, God brought those three who were involved in the fall: Adam, Eve, and Satan. God's judgment was focused on the serpent. God said to the serpent, "And the Lord God said unto the serpent, Because thou hast done this, thou art cursed above all cattle, and above every beast of the field; upon the belly shalt thou go, and dust shalt thou eat all the days of thy life: And I will put enmity between thee and the woman, and between thy seed and her seed; it shall bruise his head, and thou shalt bruise his heel." (Genesis 3:14-15). In the original Hebrew language Bible, this Scripture started with the word, "Enmity!" to emphasize that Satan is an enemy, not a friend. It reads; "Enmity, I will put between you and the woman." Enmity means an unfriendly disposition, hatred. The Lord strongly said that Satan is our enemy. Satan cannot be our friend. What do we have to do with the Enemy? We must fight against him, beat him to the death, and win.

There is a saying: "Hate the sin, yet do not hate the sinner." We should not hate the human being, but we should hate evil and sin. There should be no negotiation or compromise with evil and sin. The problem of Eve and Adam was that they mistook the Enemy as a friend and took his advice.

The phrase, "there will be enmity between Satan and the woman," means that human history, which is intermingled with God's redemptive history, would be a continuous battle between evil and human beings. That was the predicament of human history after the fall. Life after the fall was a continuous struggle with the evil forces.

Service, 1977, http://www.ichc.org/scratchpad/a44.htm. (accessed on August 20, 2011).

Failure.

Separation.

Sorrow.

Division.

Conflict.

Death.

The story of human origin is a dark picture. It seems like a dark, long tunnel that has no end.
However, look straight ahead to see the light beyond the tunnel.
Genesis 3: 15 gives light after the long and dark tunnel.
In the previous verse, the word *human* is taken as a collective, which includes all human beings. But the word returns to a singular in this verse: "And between you and your offspring and *hers*". *"Hers" in this verse means the offspring of the first human being and it was* singular as Paul translated "seed", which is the one-person Jesus Christ. Paul in Galatians 3:16, 19 explained that 'seed' as singular and it meant Jesus who was born as the descendant who was promised in time of Genesis 3:15.

From the moment of human beings' fall and great misery, God had already planned to send Christ through the channel of the human seed, the mother of Jesus, Mary. God planned to save the world and restore the human condition of happiness. Therefore, Genesis 3:15 is called the "primitive gospel"; it foreshadows the gospel of saving through Jesus Christ. That hope shines like a morning star in the dark sky.

Strike the Heel, yet Crush the Head

In this primitive gospel, God revealed two important truths.
First, Satan will strike Christ's "heel."
A seed of Eve, one man, crushing the head of the serpent, and a serpent striking the heel of one man!

You can imagine this picture similar with one of the scene of the Lord of the Ring when a boy fought with the force of evil.

This is a primitive way of expressing that Christ will suffer death on the cross. When Satan hurt Christ on the cross, it appeared that Christ was defeated. But, Satan was hurting only the "heel" of Christ. It is not pretty picture that described in verse 15 of Genesis Chapter three, which are the story of first human, Adam & Eve's fall and the judgment of God to the human and the Satan.

Likewise, even when you are in trial and have deep depression or difficulties, even when you feel that evil has overcome you and your grief becomes so intense that you feel that you are a complete failure, Satan is just striking your heel.

Second, "He will crush your head." As Christ was resurrected, He crushed the head of Satan.

Satan has no heart; he has only a big head that is crafty, highly intelligent, and clever. In his head, Satan has all sorts of tricks and tactics to deceive and to destroy. If we just use our strength and intelligence, we can never win against Satan. But, thankfully, Christ crushed the headquarters of Satan and inflicted fatal damage by His resurrection. When Jesus prayed with the troubled mind because of his struggling for the coming death, crowds, include some Greeks national, heard voice of thunder. They said it had thundered; others said an angel had spoken to him. Jesus talked to them, "This voice was for your benefit, not mine. Now is the time for the judgment of the world; now the prince of the world will be driven out. But I will draw all men to Myself when I am lifted up from the earth." (John 12: 30-32, author' paraphrase) Death is the strongest enemy to us that make us failure. It also brings the dark shadow of death. It brings sorrow, meaningless, trouble in our minds. So, Paul said in the 1st Corinthian 15: 55, "Where, O death, is your victory? Where, O death, is your sting?" When the power of death approaches us, we feel crushing defeat and terror.

However, Christ crushed the Satan' head and overcame the power of death by His resurrection. When Christ's disciples were depressed, fearful, and occupied by anxiety, Jesus encouraged them by saying, "Be courageous, even though you are going to be in tribulation. I have the victory over the world" (John 17: 33, author's paraphrase).

With the encouragement from the gospel Paul expressed his confidence of the victory over the power of death in his letter to the Romans. "Nay, in all these things we are more than conquerors through him that loved us. For I am persuaded, that neither death, nor life, nor angels, nor principalities, nor powers, nor things present, nor things to come, Nor height, nor depth, nor any other creature, shall be able to separate us from the love of God, which is in Christ Jesus our Lord." (Romans 8:37–39, KJV).

For Reflection and Discussion

1. What was the consequence of the first human beings, Adam and Eve, giving into temptation? What did humankind experience when they fell, especially in the relationship with God and other people?
2. What is the nature of our enemy, Satan? What are his tactics for leading us to tragedy? How did Satan beat the first human beings? Is there a similar tactic that Satan uses to bring us down?
3. What are the aspects of Satan's temptation in our modern culture? What does this modern culture promote that comes from Satan? In your daily struggle with Satan, what is the first thing you should do to win, victory?
4. What can you learn about the nature of human beings from the story of Leonardo da Vinci's painting of The Last Supper? Is human being originally good or evil?
5. Is evil, the temptation, bigger than God? Who ultimately controls and sovereigns our lives, our histories, and the cosmos? Why is it important to know that Satan cannot defeat Christ and that there is a limit to how much he can hurt us? When humankind lost hope after the fall, what did God plant in His promise of the primitive gospel (Genesis 3:15)?
6. Memorize Genesis 3:15 and connect it with Galatians 4:4. What can you learn about Jesus from Genesis 3:15? In your time of frustration or failure, what do you see? Hope or despair? How can you see hope in the midst of a dark reality?

God's unchangeable promise of love showed in the beautiful rainbow
Genesis 9: 1-17

[6] God is faithful to His promise, therefore, God is trustful and His faithfulness will not disappoint us. Once saved, forever saved! With His compassionate love and sincerity, He will keep our relationship with Him as a Father to His children forever.

"Covenant" is a word that is derived from the word, "Cut". In ancient times, when God wants to make a promise, he wants us to sacrifice the animals, especially a ram. When they give the burnt offering, they should

---

6   Felix R. Paturi, Die Grossen Ratsel Unserer WeltBuchumschlaggestaltung, 1971, 215.

cut the animal in halves. As they offer the burnt- offering, God gives them a promise. So, the covenant relationship established when we cut the offering into halves as a symbol that we offer thoroughly ourselves to God. It continually used when God renewed and refreshed the vision with His people. When God renewed His promise to Abraham in Genesis chapter 15, He used the word, 'Covenant'. This wonderful concept of the covenant described beautifully after the severe judgment of God. Why? It was because only God could hold the end of the covenant and mankind found impossibility of keeping the promise.

The concept of the covenant arrives in the first book of the Bible, which portrays the days of Noah and the Flood. In this story, God showed us His regrets twice. He first regretted that He created the human species. His first regret comes in the passage: Genesis 6:6, wherein it says: "The Lord saw that the wickedness of man was great in the earth, and that every imagination of the thoughts of his heart was only evil continually. And the Lord was sorry that he had made man on the earth and it grieved Him in His heart." God was sorrowful about the cruelty and corruption of human being, because it was against God's righteous nature. I assume that many parents have experienced same kinds of emotion as God experienced in the days of the Flood.

God regrets again over the creation of humans just after He brought the judgment with the flood. He felt great pain when He saw the suffering and agony of human beings. He said, "I will never again curse the ground because of man. Neither will I ever again destroy every living creature as I have done."

There was no hope for human beings in Noah's day, yet God planned to reshape human beings through one man, Noah. God reaffirmed His everlasting covenant for the human race through Noah. And God expressed His faithfulness on His covenant in a very strong and visual way - through a rainbow. After the flood was over, Lord addressed to Noah: "Behold, I establish my covenant with you and your descendants after you, and with every living creature that is with you. Never again shall all flesh be cut off by the waters of a flood, and never again shall there be a flood to destroy the earth. This is the sign of the covenant, which I make between Me and the earth. When I bring clouds on the earth and a rainbow is seen in the clouds, I will remember my covenant. When the rainbow comes on the clouds, I will look upon it and remember the everlasting covenant.

As the beautiful rainbow appeared on the sky, God repeated to Noah to imprint His covenant with humans firmly, "And God said, This is the token of the covenant which I make between me and you and every creature that is with you, for perpetual generations." (Genesis 9: 12, KJV)

God has a strong provision for His people, not because of our faithfulness to Him, but because of God's faithfulness to us. This is, indeed, the powerful foundation of God's covenant with His people.

Before I tell the story of Noah's flood and the covenant in the rainbow, allow me to talk about general concept of covenant in Christianity.

In our contracts, both parties have responsibilities and rights. But in the covenant of God, God always takes the initiative when determining the responsibilities and rules of His promise. The promise is also kept in His name because the promise that made is concrete and confirmed. The promise will not change because God is loyal to His promise, His Covenant. A covenant is a strong confirmation that God will absolutely keep His promise. Therefore, He will always hold up His end of the bargain.

How many times have you been disappointed when your friends and others have broken their promises? How many times have you disappointed about yourself because you couldn't keep your promise? This question convicts me of my inconsistency. I feel bad about this. However, it is good to know that God is faithful in keeping His covenant although we could fall off.

The covenant relationship between God and Israel is the central focus of all of the Old Testament. In the book of Hosea, God revealed Himself as both the Husband and the Father of Israel and gave them the privilege to claim their rights as legitimate spouse and/or son, depending on the covenant relationship in this particular passage of Scripture. It said, "How shall I give you up, Ephraim! How shall I deliver you, Israel? Mine heart is turned within me; my repentings are kindled together." (Hosea 11:8, KJV)

The entire panorama of events of Israelites showed that they failed to keep their promise with God, repeatedly. However, God in His faithfulness redeemed the Israelites; pursued the Israelites and consistently renewed His covenant with them. The book of Hosea described this so well. Hosea did not have a faithful wife. She kept on running away from him. However, Hosea told her, "Therefore, I will hedge up her way with thorns; and I will build a wall against her, so that she cannot find her paths. She will pursue her lovers but not overtake them, and she shall seek them, but shall not find them. Then she shall say, 'I will go and return to my first husband, for it was better with me then, than now.' And there she shall answer as in the days of her youth as at the time when she came out of the land of Egypt. And in that day, says the Lord, you shall call me, 'My husband'." (Hosea 2: 6-7, 14-16) Although his wife was unfaithful, Hosea kept the marriage covenant with his wife faithfully. Likewise, God's covenant with Israel would never break on behalf of the frailty of human being.

In the book of Romans, Paul wrote in regard prophesy of salvation of His covenant people. Paul said, "For I would not, brethren, that ye should be ignorant of this mystery, lest ye should be wise in your own conceits; that blindness in part is happened to Israel, until the fullness of Gentiles be come in. And so all Israel shall be saved: as it is written, There shall come out of Sion the Deliverer, and shall turn away ungodliness from Jacob: For this is my covenant unto them, which I shall take away their sins. As concerning the gospel, they are enemies for your sakes: but as touching the election, they are beloved for the father's sakes. For the gifts and calling of God are without repentance. For as ye in times past have not believed God, yet have now obtained mercy through their unbelief. "(Romans 11: 25-30, KJV)

By the concept of the New Covenant, we Christians are the "Covenant People" So, we can substitute the word, "Israel" as "God's covenant people". The covenant with Noah foreshadowed the New Covenant of Our Lord, Jesus Christ. At the Lord's Supper, Jesus Christ made a new covenant with His blood. Jesus Christ said: "And he said unto them, This is my blood of the new testament, which shed for many.". (Mark14: 24, KJV) As we abide in His new covenant, God will always keep His promise to us and give us hopeful life according to the new covenant.

Recognizing the Lord's Guidance in time of difficulty: Discerning God's Direction
Genesis 35: 1-21

The proper title of today's story would be, "Discerning God's will in Crisis", I have a few subtitles for today's story. They are: 'Going a little further', 'Bethel- El-bethel', and 'Where is the safest place?'

To make a firm connection with the story in Genesis chapter 35 and our own real life situation, I would like to pose for a moment and ask you questions and do the imagination.
- What place is the most memorable in your life?
- Draw images of your life's journey and mark one place that you cannot forget because it was so meaningful and memorable in your life.

Discerning God's would not be easy. Searching God's will for our lives sometimes lead us to frustration and uncertainty. Here are some general principles:

1. Listen to what the Scriptures tell you personally.
2. When you pray to God, the Holy Spirit will give you peace and confidence in your mind to approve that you make a right choice.
3. Carefully discern God's will by observing God's guiding Hand in every circumstance.

There was an unusual circumstance to Jacob's life journey in the story of Genesis chapter 35. This story tells us the wisdom of choosing the safe place to settle and discovering God's will.

The most memorable place for Jacob was 'Bethel,' because it was the place where he experienced God's presence in his most desperate moment. To refresh your memory, I would like to recount briefly the story of Bethel. In Genesis 28: 10-22, we can see that Jacob left the home for the first time in his life. He had enjoyed a comfortable life under the care of his mom and dad. But now he had to leave his home. He was not just leaving home, he was fleeing from his furious brother, Essau. En route to his safety, he reached a certain place in the middle of the wilderness. The sun had set, so he remained there for the night. As he prepared to sleep, he took a stone and used it as his pillow. It was a hard/cold stone-pillow instead of the soft/warm pillow at the home of his parents. Take a moment and think about Jacob, who had to stay overnight in the middle of the wilderness, resting on a stone pillow. I can think of these following words to explain the situation of Jacob. He was tired, sorrowful, anxious for the future, lonely and cold.

Over there in his unusual circumstance, Jacob had a dream while he slept. God appeared to him and promised: "I will bless all the people on the earth through you and your offspring. I am with you and will watch over you wherever you go. I will not leave you until I have done what I have promised you." Here was God's guaranteed promise of protection and provision for Jacob. In Jacob's most stressful moment, God confirmed His presence in Jacob's life and made a covenant with him. Jacob never expected that God would be in the wilderness. Yet Jacob found that God was right there in the desert unexpectedly. When Jacob awoke, he announced that place as "Bethel", which has same meaning of "House of God". Since then, the very location of the wilderness became known as "Bethel".

So to Jacob, Bethel was the place where God appeared to him in his worst distressful moment. It was the place Jacob received the covenant relationship with God. It was the place that he first had the amazing dream of an angel descending and ascending on a ladder that reached to heaven. Jacob could not forget Bethel throughout his life.

Do you have your own Bethel? It would not necessarily to be a specific location. It could be either memorable event that had changed your life or an event that represents a landmark of your life.

Now, let us go back to today's story. After twenty years of service at Laban, his uncle's house, Jacob came back home to Canaan. When he returned to his home, he had to settle an outstanding problem that he cheated his twin brother Essau. Once again, God helped Jacob in a strange way and saved his life. Then, according to God's command and Jacob's vow, where Jacob supposed to settle? It was Bethel, the place where God appeared to him in time of trouble. Yet, Jacob settled at Shechem. It was located on the way to Bethel, about 30 miles. If we drove by car, the distance would be maximum half an hour driving. If we walk by foot and take the flocks of sheep, this journey would take a few days, yet it was not a very long way to go on those days. If Jacob went a little further, he would have settled in the place that God had made His covenant with Jacob, which is Bethel.

After enduring the long journey of his life Jacob was too tired that he just wanted to settle at any safe haven. *We can understand that. However, if only he had thought more of his life and his covenant with God, Jacob should had gone a little further distance and should had settled at Bethel. If only he had discerned God's will more clearly, he would have returned to Bethel.*

However, Jacob did not follow God's words and found a safe haven in Shechem. Why did Jacob decide to do this? It was because Shechem was a cultured and a convenient city. Shechem means 'safely arrived'. The meaning of the city alone prompted Jacob to regard this city as a safe place to settle. Although Jacob thought it was a safe place, see what happened to Jacob's family there?

Jacob' only one daughter, Dinah was raped by the son of the Schecemites' ruler there. Upon learning that their sister Dinah had been defiled, Jacob's sons were filled with grief and fury. But they numbered only eleven men. And the Schecemites were strong tribes that had a strong sense of allegiance. To make a long story short, Jacob's sons deceitfully suggested that their sons to get circumcised since the son of the Schecemite's ruler was fall in love with Dinah and wanted to get married. Simeon and Levi, Dinah's direct brothers took the sword and attacked the city and wiped out every young man in the Shechemites' city. The brothers then took Dinah back with them to Jacob. Because of Jacob's sons' revenge, the surrounding cities were terrified of Jacob's tribe. But Jacob feared for the revenge of the surrounding city tribes and said, "Look, we are few and if they join forces against me and attack me, I and my house will be destroyed". Now you can see what happened in the place that they labeled as a safe place. Was Shechem a safe place as the name implies? It was never a safe place for him. Instead Jacob experienced trouble, because he didn't follow the will of God. He should have gone a little further to settle at the real haven for him, which is Bethel.

Jacob chose his final resting place by its physical outlook. Although Shechem was a cultured city, it should not be the city of choice according to God's covenant. If he traveled a little further distance to Bethel, Jacob would not have encountered trouble of hurting his precious daughter and surrounded by hostile enemies.

God appeared to Jacob once again when he offered himself to God and gave him clear direction and said, "Jacob, see, Shechem is not a safe place for you, although it looked like it was. Now, go up to Bethel and settle there. It was the place where I helped you in the time of your trouble. Arise, go up to Bethel and let us renew our covenant. " Now Jacob got the sense back and was going a little further to reach the land of covenant. He was like a prodigal son returning back his loving Father.

Jacob remembered God's covenant when he was in the trouble.

Then, he recommitted his life to follow God's will. Therefore, it is important to remember where God's covenant was made with us in our time of trouble.

Remember your Bethel, your spiritual home with God. Go and return to your Bethel and settle there. God's blessing will be with you there. That is the truly the place of haven for you and your family.

Over there, Jacob did three things in preparation for traveling to Bethel for worship.

First, he got rid of all foreign gods. Secondly, he purified himself.

Thirdly, he changed his clothes. Eventually, Jacob and his family arrived in Bethel and built an altar. Jacob now called that place as 'El Bethel', which means, 'God of Bethel'. By building this altar, Jacob evidently wanted to inscribe in his heart the event that he had primarily received mercy and grace from God. Now, the covenant relationship with God was reestablished and renewed.

Throughout the former life of Jacob, only God fulfilled His part of covenant, Jacob did not. Jacob forgot his promises in the most time of his life. But now when he returned to Bethel, Jacob finally fulfilled his obligation to God. Through this fulfillment, Jacob again experienced God's presence. He also experienced God as a living God. Here, God revealed His name as 'El Shaddai', which means 'God who is all sufficient and all nourishing'. (Verse 11) Our God is God who and nourishes us in provides us sufficiently every moment of our lives.

With the today' story, I would like to recommend you that:

1. Remember your Bethel. Always remember the event and the place God had first established personal relationship with you.
2. Draw near to God in any time of trouble to receive His mercy and help. Don't be afraid to seek God, for He is not holding your back and He will be there for you in time of trouble.
3. Focus on God's covenant with you instead of failure.
4. Move a little further to settle at the house of God, then you will find God of Bethel and you can call that place as "EL-Bethel".
5. Trust that your God will provide sufficiently for you and He will meet all of your practical needs, most of all He will guide your life as the good shepherd guide his sheep to the green pastures. (Psalm 23)

The Bright Morning of Jacob Jacob changed as a new person, Israel
Genesis 32:22-32

There is a time that we even could not pray because we are depressed deeply and grieving. But God will be with us even at that very moment closely as a mother who stays overnight with her baby when her baby groans with sickness. It is the promise of God Romans Chapter 8 says: 'The Spirit helps us in our weakness. We do not know what we ought to pray for, but the Spirit Himself intercedes for us with groans that words can't express. And he who searches our hearts know the mind of the Spirit, because the Spirit intercedes for the saints in accordance with God's will." Genesis chapter 32 showed that God hears us and intercedes our life to lead his people to the righteous way.

The summary of principle that we find in this chapter would be like this:

1. The darkness of night, the inner turmoil of our lives, is the prelude to the bright morning that would give you the peace of mind.
2. It hurts, really hurts when God deals justly with us. But, if we let Him prevail in our life, God will reward us with the bright morning of the soul. So, do not become filled with despair at the time of hardship. Look to the future with a positive attitude. God will deal mercifully with you. Let God prevail in your life. Amen
3. Real blessings come to us when we are transformed into new creatures of God. This truth echoes when Jesus said, "Blessed are the poor in spirit because the kingdom of God is theirs."

Is there a conversion experience in the Old Testament Era? That is a controversial and theological question. Conversion has two sides: one negative and one positive. First thing should happen is the recognition of sin and repentance. It is not so pleasant to go through this process, yet without this no one can experience and move toward the positive transformation and have an experience of the joy of salvation and real peace in the spirit.

The passage today is the narrative story about Jacob's mystical experience in the Jabbok stream, located in the upper part of the Jordan River. There, he encountered God in a very interesting and mystical way. This story portrays a man who was in the deep darkness because of his dilemma. It also describes a man who was struggling alone because of his inner conflicts resulting from relationships and anxiety. All through the night, he was wrestling, praying, questioning, tossing and struggling with his inner problems of sin, fear, distress and depression. It should have been a painful night for him because he thought that he was struggling all alone. However, God was struggling with him and Godly intervention enabled Jacob to face the bright morning.

This story presents itself almost like a legend of Israel, who is the ancestor of the Jews. It is similar with the story of ancient Greek legend. However, this story gives us a profound theological doctrine; a simple but very essential doctrinal issue, which is the issue of the conversion experience of one human being who was in a desperate moment. It also tells that there is a spiritual struggling, painful, and trouble-tossed dark night of a soul before one person receives spiritual blessings. It assures that the bright morning and the final victory will surely come to God's chosen and beloved children. This image gives us a sense of hope of victory in any circumstances that echoes what Romans 8:31 say, "If God is for us, who can be against us. In all these things, we are more than conquerors through Him who loves us."

Jacob's pilgrimage of life is a picture of one human being who struggles with fate and overcomes fate to achieve the final success. He was born as a second son of his family. In the middle- eastern Asian society, especially in the ancient period, position in the family meant a lot. The second son could not receive any inheritance or blessings from his parents. As a second son there was no opportunity to inherit blessings from his father. However, Jacob never gave up the blessings from his father. He did not render his life to fate and the human condition because he believed that God would help in any circumstances if he did his best. He never despaired.

However, in chapter 32 of Genesis, Jacob was in a very depressive and stressful situation. When I read Genesis Chapter 32 Verse 7 which the phrase that says, "In a great fear and distress", caught my attention. The King James Version translates the passage like this: "Jacob was greatly afraid and distressed." Modern people have many problems caused by stress. Stress can affect their lives seriously. It even could damage their health. When I read about the distress of Jacob, I was amazed to know that here was a man in the Bible who lived in an ancient time and suffered with a stress problem. Stress is, therefore, not only the problem of modern people but also a common problem of human beings at any time in history.

In psychology stress is defined as anything that threatens us, prods us, scares us, worries us, thrills us and it is anything that pushes us and gives tension. We are all under stress every day. It is necessary for us to move, think and work. The only problem is when that stress is more than we can bear with it. Now, in Jacob's situation, the tension was much more than he could handle.

Why, then, was he distressed? What was the cause of his distress? First of all, the root of the distress was Jacob's fear of death because Esau threatened Jacob's life. The passage said that Jacob was greatly afraid of his brother Esau. In returning to Cannon, Jacob knew that he would have to face Esau. Twenty years earlier Esau had vowed to kill Jacob because of Jacob's deception. As he came closer to his homeland, Jacob became more anxious because of his memory of Esau's anger. Jacob thought about the man of a hairy and strong hunter was waiting for revenge with his sharp sword. So, Jacob wanted to do all his best to pacify with his brother. Jacob sent a messenger to see what was going on in his brother's domain. When the messenger came back and reported that his brother Esau was coming to meet him with 400 strong men, Jacob thought that his brother was going to kill him and destroy his whole family.

What is fear? It is the cry of alarm raised by senses, which act as guardians of the body. When we sense danger, our organism is put in the position of defense. Fear is the natural response to danger. Without fear no organism could survive. Not only does everyone fear, but also all should fear. We sometimes misunderstand that Christianity does not allow fear. However, the Bible never condemns fear. Instead, Bible simply tells us how to overcome fear. Jacob's fear was caused by the threat of death. There is only one universal fear among all living beings and that is the fear of death. However, in a strict sense, one must be a human in order to feel it. The animal knows pain and fears it. But human beings alone are able to project themselves into the future and know the deep mystery of death, and therefore, human species suffer more than other species because of the fear of death. Human knows that death means 1) separation from loved ones and farewell forever; and 2) it means the end. To human, death is more fearful because they know that it would bring pains of the last agony. Even Jesus Christ, the Son of God was afraid of the 'last agony'. He was also deeply distressed and troubled before the crucifixion. He asked His disciple, "My soul is overwhelmed with sorrow to the point of death, so stay with me." And He prayed to God, "Abba Father, if possible, take this cup away from me."

Due to his fear of death, Jacob was depressed so much. Now, Jacob was showing significant symptoms of depression: 1) withdrawal from people and activities; 2) Loss of pleasure and enjoyment of life; 3) a feeling of sadness; 4) disappointment and loneliness; 5) a sleeping disturbance. (Verses 24, 13, 21, 22) In this stressful situation, it is difficult to find a way out. However, Jacob did three things.

First, he prayed to God in his time of crisis. Prayer is a great power source and it is our privilege. Philippians Chapter 4:4-7 says, "Rejoice in the Lord always, I will say again rejoice. Do not be anxious about anything. By prayer and petition and with thanksgiving, present your request to God. And the peace of God, which transcends all understanding, will guard your hearts and minds in Christ Jesus."

Secondly, he depended upon the promise of God (verse 12). In Jacob's prayer, Jacob not only requested his need, he also stood on the promise of God. Jacob petitioned, "Lord, you promised me that you would stay with me and protect and lead my life. Now, I need your help. So, save my life from my brother's hand according to your promise."

Most importantly of all, after the wrestling with God, Jacob recovered from his depression because God Himself came down and helped him. Now this is the story. In verses 22-24, we can find that Jacob stood all night alone. He sent his whole family and all his possessions over the stream and he stayed behind the river by alone. How awful it is to be so lonesome! Jacob was like a lonely bird left alone in the big forest at night. He was like a Psalmist who sang, "My heart is in anguish within me, the terrors of death assail me, fear and trembling have beset me, horror has overwhelmed me and I have said, 'Oh, that I had the wings of dove! I would fly away and be at rest.'" Have you ever been in a mood like this or found yourself in similar situation?

Anxiety and distress caused him to have a sleepless night. One of the worst pains is a sleeping disorder. It is not amusing at all. It surely is a torture. God gives sound sleep to those who rest in His Peace. What is the aloneness of Jacob in front of Jabbok stream telling us today?

It tells us the limitation of human wisdom and power. Jacob had a strong will power. He had never felt any task to be impossible before. However, even Jacob now faced the limitations of human beings.

It also tells us that human being have stand before God alone. This story of Jacob's aloneness in front of Jabbok River is allegorical picture of life. The Jabbok River can be as the 'river of death', 'sin', or 'human limitation' Canaan was the Promised Land to the Israelite and it could symbolize the life in God's promised heavenly realm in our current life or our home in heaven in the future. Jacob yearned to go to his homeland for twenty years, and now he was right there just few miles away. The homeland, for which he desired, was just across the small rapid stream. All of his family already cross over the Jabbok stream and was over there on the other side, yet Jacob could not cross over the stream. There were a lot of people around him, but no one knew what Jacob was going through. Furthermore, nobody could help him to cross the stream and get into his treasured land. As a Danish philosopher expressed, Jacob was like a lonely man among the crowd. All human beings must face this problem at some point of their lives because we are born alone and will go alone. This time should be a hard time, but it is a time when God can work within Jacob's life and really help him.

When Jacob stood alone in the presence of God, God Himself visited Jacob. As a result, Jacob experienced a dramatic conversion. During the lonesome, desperate night, 'a man', who approached Jacob, wrestled with him till daybreak. Imagine that you are in the situation of Jacob. It is a dark night, you are alone in the forest and the dark river is in front of you and an unknown man is approaching to you. It should be a frightening moment. But, to continue, Jacob held the waist of this unknown man and wrestles with him all night.

This picture of wrestling looks funny. Doesn't it? I cannot understand what Jacob was doing. But I know that Jacob was in desperate need. It was quite questionable who the man was. But the Scripture gives some clues. Hosea 12: 14 say, "The man was an angel. And Jacob's confession says "The man was God Himself." Jacob said, "I saw God face to face, yet my life is spared." (Verse 30) To sums up these factors, I can say that the man who wrestled with Jacob all night was God who appeared as the human form of an angel. We can call this as apparition. 'A man' could be the 'Pre-Incarnation of Jesus Christ'. Jesus Christ, as the God the Son, stayed within Jacob in the time of his desperate need. Jesus not only stayed there, but also struggled with Jacob.

Help comes from above! When we are so down, we even couldn't pray, yet the hands of God are always strong enough to hold our hands and escort us to the Land of Promise through the valley of death. As it was said in Romans 8: 26-27[7], The Spirit of God prays for us lift us up. At this time God's presence showed in the form of a man. God, the Trinity presence was there with one person Jacob.

When Jacob couldn't do anything, and faced human limitation, God Himself came down to help him and wrestled with his problems.

What happened when God wrestled with Jacob? Two things happened to Jacob's life at that night.

First, Jacob hurt in his hip. Jacob desperately needed help and so he held the man firmly and would not let him go. When the man found that He could not overpower Jacob, the man touched the socket of Jacob's hip. Jacob's hip was misplaced and Jacob became disabled. When God deals with you, you can be hurt. Sometimes it could make you disable person temporary.

Second, Jacob's name was changed as Israel. Jacob asked the man to give him blessing. The man answered to Jacob, 'since you ask the blessing, I want to know your name. 'How do you call your name?' Jacob answered, 'I am Jacob'. Jacob means deceiver or cheater. Jacob cheated to obtain blessings at his youth age. And later, his uncle cheated Jacob for 14 years of his life. Cheating and cheated! It was his life cycle. Jacob carried the name 'cheater' all of his life. Who in the world want to carry the name cheater? God changed his name as Israel and it has two profound meanings. The first meaning is that God has changed the person. Israel is composed with two words; Ishra-EL. in the Hebrew language, Ishra is defined as a prince and EL means God. Hence, Jacob became the prince of God, Ishra-EL.

---

[7] In the same way, the Spirit helps s in our weakness. We do not know what we ought to pray for, but Spirit himself intercedes for us with groans that words cannot express. And he who searches our hearts know the mind of the Spirit, because the Spirit intercedes for the saints in accordance with God's will. (NIV)

In the New Testament concept, the moment that Jacob's name changed as Israel could be a moment of 'Born-again' or 'Transformation'. He was changed as a new creature; the cheater became the prince of God. God transformed Jacob's life by grace. Changing a name does not only mean changed in a literal sense, but also a complete change of character. Indeed, it means a change in the whole human being. Jacob's real blessing was the experience of conversion as God had changed his name to Israel. In the Hebrew traditional dictionary, it gives a very detailed linguistic interpretation of Israel that could be spelled as 'Isahr- EL'. 'Isahr' means prevail and 'EL' means God. So, Second interpretation of the meaning of Israel is 'Let God prevails'. That interpretation is in tune with verse 28. Let me read this verse, "Your name will no longer be Jacob, but Israel, because you have struggled with God and with men and have overcome. The verb in verse 28, 'overcome' could be best illustrated when we compare to a father wrestling with his little son. The Father is stronger, but he just lets the son win. So, when Jacob overcame in the wrestling it was because God let him won and God hit Jacob's hip. So, actually God prevailed and overcame in Jacob's life.

The first and the second definition of the name, Israel, have some continuity. If you let God prevail in your life, you will receive the blessing of God that transforms you into a new creature, a prince of God.

After God had changed Jacob's name, Jacob became a total new being and a bright morning opened upon Jacob's life. It was the dawning of a new soul. Jacob called the place of this occurrence 'Peniel,' because he encountered God face to face and his life was spared. Peniel means 'I encountered God's face'. The passage in verse 31 describes the beautiful sunrise at the Jabbok River; "The sun rose above Jacob as he passed Peniel." It was an allegorical description of a new dawn that began for Jacob when he encountered God's face. The verse describes not only the beauty of nature in the sunrise in the Jabbok stream, but also the brightness of the grace of God that shines within the man who encountered God. Verse 31 continues, "He was limping."

As you look at the back of this man, you could see that he was hurt. He limped, was disabled and looked miserable. However, if you look directly at his face, the bright morning sunshine which was the grace of God shone upon his face. As the grace of God shone upon Jacob, the peace of God stayed with him. As God's grace shone upon Jacob's life, all his fear, anxiety and distress disappeared.

CHAPTER 2
JESUS CHRIST, MESSIAH, GIVES HOPE MESSAGE

---

[8] Presentazion di Michelle Prisco, Raffaello, Classici Dell'Arte, Rizzoli Editore Milan, TAV. LXIV.

The Awesome concept that God brought at Christmas
John 1:14

I WAS THINKING THE MOST IMPORTANT THING about Christmas and that is: God came down to our level. Christmas is important because it is the day the world savior Christ was born and God came down to us, not just to visit, but to dwell among us and be with us.

Jesus Christ was born in the manger, a very lowly place where the horses and cattle smelled; as it was written in the books of prophesy. The eternal God, prince of peace and king of kings, comforter and most of all, savior of the world came into the manger. Most of the people in the world celebrate the birth of Christ in these days. However, Christ's birth seemed very insignificant to people on those days because he was born in a very insignificant place. Not many people recognized Christ's birth except only few groups of shepherds, Wiseman, and few Jewish who came to visit him. The historian Luke described the long story of the birth of Christ with those historical situations. Let me expose few verses of Luke chapter 2: "In those days Caesar Augustus issued a decree that a census should be taken of the entire Roman world. This was the first census that took place while Qurinios was governor of Syria. With his decree everyone went to his own town to register." Augustus means honored and it was named only for the emperor. In fact, Caesar was the first person who owned the name of Augustus. If there were a newspaper, the top news in the Headline would be, "Caesar Augustus, the first emperor, made Roman road to the world: The decree of census for all Roman world" Augustus was the almost raised himself up to the level of god. It means honorable and the name Augustus could be given to only one person, the first legitimate empire of Rome. It was time that Augustus laid the foundation of long lasting, millennium empire of Rome. So, Augustus got all attention of the world not Jesus because he was born just in the corner of country town Bethlehem. That was how Joseph went up to Bethlehem and Jesus was born through Mary in the town of David, Bethlehem. Joseph and Mary had long journey when Mary conceived Jesus with the Holy Spirit.

By the time when they arrived at Bethlehem, Mary was expecting baby any moment. But nobody gave them a room. There was no room for the birth of Jesus. I remember when my family traveled from Texas to Florida to see the Walt-Disney World. We arrived at night. We were tired. We just wanted to get in any room available, motel, inn whatever offered. But as I drove in the town, I saw the sign "No vacancy". I was so frustrated and tired as I looked for the place to stay a night. You might have experienced this when you traveled Europe.

Imagine Joseph and Mary's desperateness. Joseph might have pleaded hundred times, "Please, give me a room. My wife is pregnant and it is full" However, nobody gave them a room. Historian Luke recorded, "She gave birth to her firstborn, a son. She wrapped him swaddling clothes, and laid Him in a manger because there was no room." People were busy for their own lives had no room to concern for other's misery. However, there were someone who showed the hospitality to Mary and Joseph. Even though it was not well-equipped and just lowly manger, they welcomed Christ with warm hearts and offered the place for the birth. This event that took place in the Bethlehem has significant meaning and that is: "God came down into our level; came down to the lowest place".

Why God the creator made his only begotten Son to born in the lowest place and insignificant to the people? There are very profound truths in His incarnation.

God came down to our level.

God, the eternal creator came down to our human level not just check us, but to dwell among us. Matthew described this with simple word, "Emmanuel", which means God is with us, John described with short phrases, "The Word, who was in the beginning with God became flesh."

In a famous cathedral of Rome, a magnificent fresco radiates its beauty. Every colorful detail has been painted artfully. However, for the centuries, few visitors who went to the cathedral appreciated the magnificent paint. It was not because of the lack of mastery or beauty. It was because of its location of the art was painted at the ceiling of a high and lofty cathedral dome. Everyone tried to look up the paint on the top had a problem of eyestrain and stiff-neck. The physical discomfort prevented enjoyment of the beautiful art.

After centuries passed, someone suggested putting a large mirror just above the floor level. A sight once too far away and difficult to behold was brought down to human eye level that everyone could enjoy the beauty of the master art that was painted on the ceiling of a dome. People could seat and enjoy the splendor of the excellent painting by looking down the lower mirror.

That was exactly what God did for us on the first Christmas. The invisible God came down to us in the human level. Jesus is the image of the invisible God. No one has seen God. The ancient believed that anyone who actually saw God face to face would die. We couldn't seek for too much closeness with God. So, we keep distance from Divine. Even Moses was not allowed to look at God face by face. However, God the Son, who was within and with the God the Father, came down and revealed God.

There is an Indian proverb, "If you don't wear the other's shoes, do not think you understand them". To understand others, we have to go through what they had gone through. God came down to our level and stayed in the lowest place to understand us and help us. Paul explained this principle profoundly, "Who, being in the very nature of God, did not consider equality with God something to be grasped, but made himself nothing, taking the very nature of a servant being made in human likeness."

As a summary, I want to borrow the England preacher Surgeon's illustration about the birth of Christ. He said, "The creator who put the magnificent stars in heaven, who created moon and universe, whose age is eternal and whose hair is white like wool shrink into nothing and hung on to Mary to get His nourishment" Christ, the Eternal God the Son came down to me and asked to me, "Hi, Woo Young What's up? What' going on with you? And He understands me and loves me. What an awesome concept that God would do something like this for us. I hope tonight that each of us would come to realize and understand the full meaning of this truth.

Would you bow with me for the prayer?

"Almighty and gracious Heavenly Father, Holy and eternal God, With the overwhelming appreciation, we thank you that you showed your deep love for us by coming down to us and be present in every corner of our lives, especially in our hearts. I thank you for the savior, Jesus Christ, who was born in Bethlehem. As we celebrate the birth of our savior Jesus Christ and worship, give us your joy and peace. I pray in the name of Jesus Christ.

Immanuel

"All this took place to fulfill what the Lord had spoken by his prophet; "Behold, a virgin shall conceive and bear a son, his name shall be called Immanuel."(With means, God with Us.) (Matthew 1:23)

The four years old girl didn't want to stay alone in the dark bedroom. Mommy assured her that she wouldn't be alone. Mommy said to her, "God would be there with you." She replied, "Mommy, but I want a God that has a face!"

That child speaks for us all. Deep within our souls we long to see God up close. For many centuries, mankind stood a restless night and watched the stars in heavens to search for sign of God, longing to see Him face to face.

So, how big is God? He is big enough to create and rule an unending universe but small enough to fit in the form of newborn baby. God weighted perhaps seven pounds and six ounces that night, but he was all loving and very visible. Is there anything more visible than a baby? It was the only way we creatures of such poor vision could see Him. During World War II, a child lovingly looked at his father's picture. Looking for his return she asked her mother, "Wouldn't it be wonderful if daddy could just step our of this picture and be home?" That is what God did in Christ. Although the distance was great, He simply stepped out of the stars to be with us. "For to us a child is born, to us a Son is given, and the government will be on his shoulders. And he will be called Wonderful Counselor, Mighty God, Everlasting Father, and Prince of Peace."

God stepped out of His glorious throne to be with us today.

Let me introduce one great musician, Handel , George Frederic who compose the famous concert of Messiah. He was a professional organist in Halle Cathedral and Hamberg opera orchestra four years and won a considerable acclaim and enjoyed the 14 yrs of great success as a operatic composer. However in 1737 he lost his popularity and bankrupt and abandoned his operatic endeavors. After that, he had been depressed for five yrs and he almost abandoned his life. However, One day, God inspired him with the word of Isaiah Chapter 9, it was so encouraging word to him that the baby born in the manger is the prince of peace and the wonderful counselor, with the inspiration he composed the famous classical music piece,

"Messiah" With this he was not only saved, but also gain the his public favor and acclaim as a musician, overcome the financial difficulties as well.

Christmas message lifted him up and made him excited about the life again.

So, Jesus as a wonderful counselor would lift you up and make your life excited.

Because he would give you a wonderful encouragement, wise advice with the grace and the truth.

The Law and Grace
Matthew 5:17–18, John 1:16–17, John 8:1–11

What did Jesus say about the supreme law in the days when Judaism prevailed?

For the Israel people, keeping the law was so important because it made them a covenant people, which was their identity and belonging. They would become outcasts if they did not keep the Mosaic Law. There are many stories that tell that they are would rather choose to die than violate the law throughout the history of the people Israel; for example, Matthias against Antiochus IV, Daniel's story, or Esther's life. In the LXX version of the Bible, in Esther 4:7, Esther told God that she had not eaten food from Haman's table or drunk wine for the liberation and uplift of her spirit. Eating pork and associating with uncircumcised people were forbidden to all the people of Israel. This rule applied even to those who lived in foreign countries.

With their hope for the messianic kingdom, they anticipated for having a messianic teacher who would understand the Mosaic Law and comply with it. Isaiah 42:4 declared that the servant of Yahweh would establish justice in this earth by bringing law to the people is one example of the Israelites yearning for the Messiah who would be the advocator of the Mosaic Law.

Jesus seemed too radical and permissible to become their messiah. Jesus healed on the Sabbath without any hesitation. He healed the people at synagogue. Jesus' ministry reflected His radical view of the law, even giving the impression that He was against the law. It was obvious that Jesus was not keeping the law of Sabbath literally. This made some people misunderstand that Jesus gave them permission to break the law, which caused Jesus as the controversy person. Jesus figure never could fit to their Messianic concept.

However, Jesus did not want them to misunderstand His perspective on the law. He gave absolute respect to the Mosaic Law.

Matthew 5:17–18 reads, "Do not think that I have come to abolish the Law or the Prophets; I have not come to abolish them but to fulfill them. I tell you the truth, until heaven and earth disappear, not the smallest letter, not the least stroke of a pen, will by any means disappear from the Law until everything is accomplished." "The Law or the Prophets" in these verses means the Old Testament of the Scriptures in Jesus' day. Jesus was a law teacher who enforced Mosaic Law absolutely.

The gospels and the writing of Josephus characterized Jesus as a teacher of the people. Gospels make it clear that understanding Jesus as a teacher of the law is a part of understanding Him as the Messiah. Pinchas Lapide, an orthodox Jewish rabbi and scholar, said that Jesus was a good law keeper and therefore a good teacher of the law: "Jesus never and nowhere broke the Law of Moses, nor did he in any way provoke its infringement. In this respect you must believe me, for I know my Talmud. I suspect that Jesus was more faithful to the law than I am and I am an Orthodox Jew."[9]

When He healed the sick on the Sabbath, the day on which Jewish people are prohibited to work, how could Jesus say that He was keeping the Mosaic Law absolutely?

When Jesus said to keep the Mosaic Law absolutely, He meant to keep the law beyond the word, to keep the motivation, which was God's compassion and generosity. Here are three things to consider:

If people understood what was meant by "not even the smallest letter can pass from the Bible" in the original Hebrew text, they would understand that Jesus meant that the law should be kept by its meaning not by the literal stipulation. The smallest letters and strokes remain binding. The smallest Hebrew letter is *yod*, which almost resembles an apostrophe: '.

Ignoring the smallest letter or mixing up two similar shape of letter will change the meaning of the word a lot. It could lead to a totally opposite meaning. One of the typical examples is in Deuteronomy 6:4, "Hear, O Israel: The Lord our God is one Lord."(*Shema Yisrael: Adoniai Eloheinu Adonai Echad*) If one changes the Hebrew word *Echad* changing to *echtar* (ד: Dalet- in English sound similar with *d*, ר: Resh-in English sound similar with *r*), this verse could be translated as "God is another god." It changes the meaning totally and could lead people to misunderstand God, the only God, as an idol.

ד: Dalet (dāleth, also spelled Daleth or Daled) is the fourth letter of many Semitic alphabets

---

9   Phinhas Lapide, in Hans Kung, "Jesus in Conflict," a dialogue between Phinhas Lapide and Hans Kung, in Signposts for the Future, edited by Hans Kung (New York: Doubleday, 1978), 74–75.

ר: Resh (Arabic: look below) is the twentieth letter of many Semitic alphabets[10]

Therefore, it is important to keep the law beyond the letter.

Jews blamed Jesus that He broke the law of Judaism, yet Jesus was the one who really respected and perfectly kept the law. Jesus' teaching did not make any teaching of the Law as invalid and lower the ethical, moral standard. Instead, Jesus kept the law with the highest standard, just as He taught in Matthew 5:19: "Anyone who breaks one of the least of these commandments and teaches others to do the same will be called least in the kingdom of heaven, but whoever practices and teaches these commands will be called great in the kingdom of heaven."

Jewish traditional law focuses on loving God with all our hearts and minds, as Deuteronomy 6:4–5 says. The second commandment is to love our neighbors, as Leviticus 19:19, 19:33–34, and 22:39 say. Jewish people in Jesus' time tried hard to keep the first commandment, yet they failed to connect the first commandment to the second commandment. Most of them failed to act out God's love. However, Jesus connected these two very well and, therefore, was able to love God and human beings at the same time. Jewish people in Jesus' day were so antagonistic to Jesus because they could not connect these two important commandments of love. It is misleading to think that Jesus was against Judaism. Jesus helped them to understand the real meaning of keeping the law. For example, He spoke to one young man who was excellent in keeping the law: "Love the Lord your God with all your heart and with all your soul and with all your strength and with your entire mind; and Love your neighbor as yourself" (Matthew 22:36–40; Luke 10:27).

The highlight of Jesus as a teacher of the law took place in the Sermon on the Mount in Matthew's gospel. Jesus taught a high ethical standard as He interpreted the Mosaic Law. Jesus' application of Mosaic Law stood above that in the Judaism of His day, which gave high regard to keeping the law in the society of other covenant people. The fact was that Jesus internalized the people's motivation, which was love instead of a literal interpretation of

---

10   Hebrew alphabet - Wikipedia, the free encyclopedia en.wikipedia.org/wiki/Hebrew alphabet (accessed on September 11, 2011)

the law, and He emphasized generosity and compassionate love beyond the law and its stipulations.

Jesus' Interpretation of the Commandments

Murder

In regard the murder, Jesus said, "You have heard that it was said to the people long ago, 'Do not murder, and anyone who murders will be subject to judgment,' but I tell you that anyone who is angry with his brother will be subject to judgment. Again, anyone who says to his brother, 'Raca' [which means "contempt"] is answerable to the Sanhedrin. But anyone who says, 'You fool' will be in danger of the fire of hell" (Matthew 5:21–22).

Murder was the act of killing unlawfully. Jesus regarded speaking to or of others with disrespect and looking down on others as equal to murder. Jesus' interpretation of the law went beyond the act itself to the hearts and minds of the people. Jesus taught that anger, plots, and attempts to defraud anther would bring the same consequences as murder and would deserve capital punishment. Jesus warned that these kinds of murderers should eventually fall in hell.

Adultery

Regarding adultery, Jesus said, "You have heard that it was said, 'Do not commit adultery.' But I tell you that anyone who looks at a woman lustfully has already committed adultery with her in his heart. If your right eye causes you to sin, gauge it out and throw it away. It is better for you to lose one part of your body than for your whole body to be thrown into hell" (Matthew 5:27–29).

Jesus did not simply see the action of not committing adultery as proof of a pure heart; the motivation to commit adultery was committing adultery already. Simply looking at unclean pictures or provocative people affects the internal sensor and causes lust. Seeing is a powerful way of motivating people's lust for sin. The first woman, Eve, just looked at the Tree of Knowledge of Good and Evil, and lust imbedded in her heart. Internet sites tempt modern people powerfully. Some may have good control over their actions; however, no one could have control over their inner spirits and minds. Jesus said that even if someone did not commit adultery, lusting was a sin already and that the person deserved to be thrown into hell. Jesus seemed to hold the view of extreme stoic Judaism yet He just emphasized the motivation of hearts and minds.

Divorce

Jesus said, "It has been said, 'anyone who divorces his wife must give her a certificate of divorce. But I tell you that anyone who divorces his wife, except for marital unfaithfulness, causes her to become adulterous and anyone who marries the divorced woman commits adultery'" (Matthew 5: 31–32). Matthew explained the divorce issue in this way: "Moses permitted you to divorce your wives because your hearts were hard. But it was not like from the beginning." (Matthew 19: 8, NIV)

Divorce for the people Israel was not because of adultery. It could be just displeasing one's wife because of indecent or unpleasant things. It could have to do with the wife not cooking a good enough meal. The laws in Deuteronomy seemed favorable in the man-dominated culture. Many men took advantage of this law to marry someone whom they lusted after. However, Moses' permission to give a divorce certificate was not meant to advocate divorce. Its purpose was to protect the women who got divorced. To show the absolute holiness of the marriage covenant to His people, Jesus quoted the foundation of marriage from Genesis: "But at the beginning of creation God made them male and female. For this reason a man will leave his father and mother and be united to his wife, and the two will become one flesh. So, they are no longer two, but one. Therefore, what God has joined together, let man not separate" (Matthew 10:5–9). Jesus bluntly said that divorcing was a leading action to adultery for the divorcees. Further, divorcing except for reasons of unfaithfulness was already committing adultery.

Grace and Truth

Jesus had two purposes for teaching the law at the Sermon on the Mount. The first purpose was to raise the standard of the law beyond the law of the mind. Jesus reinterpreted Judaism as the law of love.

Jesus' teaching of the law was like a clear and pure mirror that reflected the minds and hearts of the people clearly. With His interpretation of the law, Jesus helped people seek and know who they really were. It would also help them understand that they would not reach the standard of the supreme law of Judaism, which was perfect purity, love, and transparency. That ideal was far beyond the reach of their actions.

People could fulfill the law only when they were bonded with Jesus, who fulfilled the law once for all with His redemptive sacrifice. Through the ministry in His life, Jesus showed how to keep the law and love others with God's grace.

Grace is the only way that we human beings can reach the standard of God's law. Jesus revealed grace vividly when He showed forgiveness and compassion to one misled lady in John 8:1–11. He also showed the truth of grace in John 1:1–16: From the fullness of his grace we have all received one blessing after another. For the law was given through Moses; grace and truth came through Jesus Christ." (John 1: 16-17)

People could survive the tide of the law's punishment only when they stayed in the salvation ark of our Lord Jesus. May the grace of Jesus be with you!

For Reflection and Discussion

1. How important are the law and the prophecy (the Word of God in the Old Testament) to Jesus?
2. Do you have an absolute truth that you cannot negotiate in any circumstances? Why is it important to have an absolute truth in our lives?
3. How do adultery, murder, and divorce, which are so prevalent in these modern days, affect people's lives? What actions do sinful minds cause human beings to take?
4. What was Jesus' deep motivation for keeping the Word of God absolutely? How did Jesus fulfill the promise of the prophets and the law?
5. Why did Jesus teach grace and truth? Why can human beings only be saved by grace? (John 1:14–16)
6. How can we live a balanced life with grace and truth?

Christ will give you eternal life
John chapter 3, Ecclesiastes chapter 3

Time & Eternity from Ecclesiastes chapter 3

I've met one very sincere Christian couple. They were going to have their first baby very soon. It was to be a daughter. However, something happened and the baby could not be removed from the womb and the baby died. The couple experienced tremendous sorrow and grief. They worried about the eternal destiny of the baby asked a question, "Where is our baby going to spend her time in her eternal destiny?" The mother had learned that those who never accepted Christ as their Savior would be destined to remain in a horrible place. Her question was, "Is my baby going to spend her eternity at hell?" I shared my belief and told her, "All human beings fall under the category of Adam's sin. All of them are born with sin. However, your baby and all children who were not yet exposed to the temptation of sin are innocent. Therefore, God will regard them as angels. So, your daughter will be in heaven with the Lord."

Whatever your beliefs are, we are all limited human beings and we do not know our eternal destiny and occasionally we wonder about it.

Years ago, a Polish priest named Gerogu got the Nobel Prize in literature for the book entitled, "The 25th Hour". The setting was during the period when the Germans persecuted the Jews. The main character had a last name, which was similar to a Jewish name. But, actually the man was not a Jew. Nonetheless, he was thrown into prison and separated from his family. He was faced with many troubles. In his novel, Georgu tried to describe a human being who had lost his ground of existence. He had no place to stand. The title of his novel, **The 25th Hour**, matched the story very well. All humankind is bounded in time and space. We all live in the two dimensions. If we want to live in the twenty-fifth hour, we would be like a train derailed.

In today's scriptures, Solomon explained about the "time factor" in our lives in various ways. He said, "There is a time for everything, and a season for every activity under heaven: a time to be born and a time to die."

The writer of the book of Ecclesiastes is Solomon and he wrote two wisdom literatures, one is Proverbs and the other is Ecclesiastes. In the first two chapters of Ecclesiastes, he expressed lots of his frustration and agony in a very negative way, "Meaningless! Meaningless! Everything is meaningless. What does man gain from all his labor at which he toils under the sun? All things are wearisome, more than one can articulates. The eye never has enough of seeing, or the ear its fill of hearing. There is nothing new under the sun." He asked the question, "Is there anything of which one can say, look this is something new? No! Solomon continued in aggravation and said, "Wisdom, knowledge even pleasure and hard work for the good life are all meaningless! About wisdom, 'I thought to myself, 'Look, I have grown and increased in wisdom more than anyone who has ruled over Jerusalem before me. Then I applied that wisdom to life and it worked perfectly, but I learned that this too is a chasing after the wind. Will the man who comes after me be a wise man or a fool? Yet he will have control over all the work into which I have poured my effort and skill under the Sun."

He kept on saying concerning pleasure, "I built houses for myself and planted nice vineyards, gardens, parks, and fruit trees. I hired many workers who worked for me. I also owned more herds and flocks than anyone in Jerusalem before me. I gathered silver and gold. I became greater. My heart took delight in all my work, and this was the reward for all my labor. Yet when I surveyed all that my hands had done and what I had toiled to achieve, everything was meaningless, a chasing after the wind, nothing was gained under the sun, because I must leave them to the one who comes after me."

Solomon had every privilege of life. God had blessed Solomon with wisdom and wealth. God gave him power and fame. However, Solomon complained, became aggravated and even hated life.

Becoming more aggravated and his heart began to despair. He said, 'So I hated life' I myself thought that this could not be in the Holy Bible. However, Solomon's words do not remain in his negative, pessimistic expression. Solomon progresses to the next chapter and said, "life is beautiful. There is a time for everything in life: a time for sorrow, a time for happiness, a time for failure and a time for success, because God has made everything beautiful in its time. And God has set a yearning for eternity in the hearts of men" (3:10)

Solomon became pessimistic when he recognized that humankind was limited by the time frame. No matter what they had achieved and what possessions they had, all humans had to die as it said in scripture, "There is a time to be born and a time to die." We are limited by a time frame. One of the Psalms that Moses wrote says, "Life is like an arrow in the archer's bow, it goes fast. Some people live to be 80, some live longer, but there are lots of toils and agony."

It is good to recognize the limitation of humankind by a time frame, because that realization would lead people to yearn for something long-lasting, meaningful, and furthermore, eternal. So, now returning to Solomon, Solomon later said, "Be happy, young man, while you are young, and let your heart give you joy in the days of your youth. But, remember your Creator in the days of your youth, before the days of trouble come" (Ecclesiastes 11:9- 12:1)

Although we are bounded by time and space, Jesus will give us eternal life. John 7: 37 said; "On the last day and the greatest day of the feast, Jesus stood among the crowds and said in a loud voice, 'If a man is thirsty, let him come to Me and drink. Whoever believes in Me, as Scripture has said, 'streams of water will flow from within him or her.' " In Isaiah 55:1, it says, "Come, all who are thirsty, come to the waters, and you who have no money, come and buy and eat. Buy wine and milk without money and without cost. Why spend money on what is not bread and your labor on what does not satisfy? Listen, to Me and eat what is good and your soul will delight in the richest of fare." Christ gives hope of the everlasting life.

Now, I would like to tell you the story of the Samaritan woman and Jesus. It is one of the most famous stories in the Bible. I believe that you have often heard this story. It begins in John's gospel chapter four. Now, Jesus was walking and had long journey going through Samaria, the hot desert. He was thirsty and hungry. Soon He arrived to a town in Samaria called Sychar, where there was Jacob's well. (Joseph inherited this well) Jesus was so tired that he just sat down by the well. And it was about the sixth hour; it is around noontime in our measurement of time. Jesus was so thirsty. He asked the Samaritan woman, "Will you give me a drink?" The Samaritan woman said to Jesus very unkindly, "You are a Jew and I am a Samaritan woman.

How can you ask me for a drink?" She was very unkind because Jews never associated with Samaritans. Jesus answered her, "If you knew the gift of God and who it is that asks you for a drink, you would have asked Him and He would have given you living water." Jesus is the Creator, but in this earth His nationality was Jewish and His gender was man. This woman was Samaritan, a human and a woman. There are many differences here. However, Jesus and the Samaritan woman had one common need. Both needed something to quench their thirst—Jesus needs water to quench his thirsty—this woman, spiritually. As a response for Jesus' asking for water, this woman who always came to the well of Jacob, now asked Jesus one question, "Are you greater than our father, Jacob?"

Let us take a moment to think of why a Samaritan woman, who kept on coming to Jacob's well, asked Jesus a very meaningful question: "Are you greater than our father, Jacob?" Why do you think this woman kept on coming to Jacob's well? Why had she asked Jesus, "Are you greater than Jacob?" She asked this question because she needed the water that would sustain her life, sense of belongingness, and the love that lasts forever.

In summary, this story tells us symbolically that humans have three basic needs, physical, emotional, and social sense of belongingness to a group to depend on each other; someone whom they can receive love and give love. We cannot deny these three needs, but we have to recognize the fact that even though we possesses all of those, physical, emotional, social needs , without Christ we would be still thirsty as Jesus said, "Everyone who drinks this water will be thirsty again."

Isaiah said, "Why spend money on what is not bread and expend your labor on what does not satisfy? (Isaiah 55:2) Success in one's career, personal achievement, economical stability, recognition, friendship, and a happy marriage! We value all of those physical and emotional desires and it is important to have those desires. However, as we have experienced, we get an "empty feeling" even after we obtain those things that we really wanted. We climb the mountain to reach our goals and successes. We thought that we would be perfectly happy once we had achieved those goals. But, that satisfaction does not last long. We should go further, succeed more and achieve more to quench our thirst for personal gain. It is like drinking salty water. The more you drink, the less your thirst is quenched.

I sometimes wondered, "Why can't humans be perfectly satisfied?" The answer is; that is how we are created. God made us to depend on Him for our spirituality, our eternity. As the book of Ecclesiastes said, "God has set eternity in the hearts of humankind." When were born, it was God that put the desire, the yearning for eternity in our conscious and in our subconscious. Only God, who is eternal, can quench our thirst for eternity. Jesus said, "Whoever drinks this water will be thirsty again, but whoever drinks the water I give him will never thirst. Indeed, the water I give him will become a spring of water welling up to eternal life." (John 4:13-14)

What does this mean? Why does the water that Jesus gives become a spring of water welling up to eternal life?

It means first that Christ's love is perfect, spiritual, eternal. So, Christ's love is spiritual drink for us. Human needs sincere and everlasting love. When the Samaritan woman heard about the spring of water welling up to eternal life, she asked Christ, "Sir, give me this water, so that I won't get thirsty again." Jesus told her, "Go, call your husband and come back." She replied, "I have no husband." Jesus said to her, "you are right when you say you have no husband. The fact is, you have had five husbands, and the man you now have is not your husband. What you have said is quite true" Either the woman was unfaithful or the husbands were unfaithful. Whatever the case, this woman had lots of hurts with broken marriage. As a result, she had experienced much pain. Whenever she drew water from Jacob's well, she thought about the story of Jacob who was sincere and faithful man Jacob, who loved only one woman.

As you know, Jacob worked for fourteen years for one woman, Rachel. Day and night, he fed the flocks of Rachel's father. He was given no salary, no reward for his effort. He toiled just because he loved Rachel. Jacob looked foolish to others, but to the Samaritan woman who had broken off from five husbands, Jacob was admirable because Jacob's love was sincere and faithful. This is another facet of the Samaritan woman's question to Christ, "Are you greater than Jacob? With this question, she was actually asking, "Is your love, God's love, more sincere and more faithful than Jacob's love for Rachel?" As Christ' love quenches the spirit of this woman, His love, Agape love will quench our thirst for the eternity.

When Jesus said to the woman, "I will give you springs of water welling up to eternal", Jesus meant that He would accept the woman rejected even by her tribes as God's loving children.". Jesus was saying that God welcomed the Samaritan woman who was rejected even by her tribes and accepting her as God's loving children. To the Samaritan woman, Jacob's well was not just a place to draw water; it was more than a physical well. This woman was looking for a sense of belongingness at Jacob's well. Think about why she was asking the unusual question, "Are you greater than our father, Jacob? She emphasized the fact that Jacob was her ancestor and she was one of the children of Jacob. And she noted that Jacob, himself, drank from the same well, as did his sons and his flocks and his herds as well. She also stated that Jacob handed over the well to her people, the Samaritans.

I would like to tell you the history of the relationship between the Jews and the Samaritans. Actually, the Jews and the Samaritans were the same race, the same nation. At BC 722, they were divided into two sections. The Jews inhabited the southern part of Israel, the northern territory by the Samaritans. As you know the Jewish people were very exclusive and they live in a closed society. They despised the Samaritans, even though they lived in the same country. The Jews ostracized the Samaritans and treated them as third class citizens because the Samaritans intermarried into foreign nations, especially with Assyrians. Following the invasion by Assyria into the Northern kingdom of Israel in 722 BC, the Israelites in Northern Israel, which we call Samaritans, intermarried with the Assyrians. The Jews were intolerant of the mixture of the Samaritan and Assyrian cultures. The hostility lasted for a very long time. Even after six centuries in 120 BC, when the Samaritans built a temple in their city, Gerzim, the southern Jews attacked the Samaritans and destroyed the entire temple. The Southern Jews treated the Samaritans as their worst enemy.

But, the Samaritan were not foreigners, they were Jews. They could not be Romans; they could neither be Greeks nor any other nation, because they were Jews. But at the same time, they were rejected by their own people and would not be accepted as Jewish. They were on the fringe of two different nations. And the sad fact was that Samaritans could not even have any belongingness. That is their dilemma. That was why, this woman kept on saying that "You are a Jew, I am a Samaritan woman. Our fathers, yours and mine, were Jews. You may deny it, but we belong to each other. Whenever, she came to Jacob's well she reminded herself of the fact that "I belong to Jacob" And she said to herself, "No matter what the Jewish people says, we are all the descendants of Jacob, Abraham is my ancestor."

Have you experienced rejection from others of the same race? Have you been excluded from their association and their fellowship even you live within their neighborhood? Have you been ignored because of your differences in comparison to them? Or have you excluded others who want to associate with you? " Exclusion causes a terrible, pitiful feeling. That was just what the Samaritan woman felt. She felt ostracized, excluded and alone. Do you feel ostracized, excluded even from Christian?

The need to belongingness, to be a part of something, tells us that we humans are social beings. In the famous story, *Robinson Crusoe*, Robinson Crusoe did not like people because there were many conflicts in human relationships. To resolve this problem, he went go to an isolated, distant island and lived alone. However, Crusoe learned that humans are social beings and need people around even though there were ongoing conflicts in human relationship. With this newfound insight, Robinson Crusoe came back to society. Humans need people, a group in which they can belong. Human tend to be selective. We like certain people but we do not like others. We prefer this and we do not prefer that. However, Jesus in His actions, in His words, and in His heart embraces everybody. He accepts the ones who are rejected by others. God accepts us as we are and regards us as His children. In Christ Jesus, we drink of His acceptance of all people and it will be a spring of water welling up to eternal life.

Thirdly, we will have eternal life in Christ, literally. The first reason that the Samaritan woman kept on coming to the Jacob's well was because the woman needed the water. It was a symbolic way of telling us that people need basic physical things. We wake up early in the morning and go to work. We work hard for our family to bring bread to the family's table. We are similar to the Samaritan woman who kept on going to Jacob's well to draw water. We are consistently needful beings. We are consuming things, at the same time; we are consumable being that would end our life as ashes.

However, Christ will give eternal life to us. We will not be bound by time when we join with His eternity. When we pass from this life, we will continue in that right path forever in eternity. We will not be bound by time. We will be living a spiritual life now and forever.

Jesus is the true bread of life. His words and actions are the water of which we can drink and lead us to eternity. If we seek only material things, we will die. There is nothing, either material or emotional things, in this world that can perfectly satisfy us nor can launch us into our eternity. However, In God, we will always have eternity. Jesus gives to us water, which becomes the spring of water that wells up and transports us to everlasting life. The everlasting life, the springing of water that last forever, is the privilege that we would possess since we become new born creatures in Christ. I pray that God would give spring of water that wells up to you today. In Jesus Name, I pray. Amen.

The Song of Victory on Passion day
Matthew 21:1-11

The beautiful music, the prelude of God's victory, was already played as the opening ceremony of redemption history started during Christ our Lord Jesus entered into Jerusalem.

Do you remember the bloody war at the Alamo in Texas when Colonel David Crocket and all of his fellow soldiers died? They lost the battle over there in Texas Alamo miserably. However, the history records that because of the sacrifice of the Soldiers at Alamo and the patriotic offering their body for the freedom, the Union of American Soldier won a victory later. Likewise, Christ's suffering and death laid the foundation for the coming victory. It is painful to even hearing Christ's suffering. However, we hear the song of the prelude of the final victory in his entering the city for the suffering.

With this passage of Passion scriptures, I would like to remind you of two things.

First, the suffering of Jesus during the week of the Passion was enormous.

Second, there was a prelude of victory before Christ's enemies surrounded Him.

While meditating on the Passion passages, I am reminded of Psalm 25:1-3: "Unto thee, O Lord, do I lift up my soul. O my God, I trust in thee: let me not be ashamed; let not mine enemies triumph over me." Although His pain was enormous, Jesus could bear the distress because He knew that He would attain victory in a few days after His suffering and crucifixion. Think about Jesus who already predicted and knew unequivocally what kind of suffering take place within hours and yet remained calm and entered Jerusalem as a king who would win the ultimate victory. He was surrounded with the song of the prelude of the final victory.

Let us review first what will happen in a few hours. What happened there when Christ suffered on the cross? The scene was in the middle of the day, but all of a sudden, the Sun lost its light and there was darkness all over the world.

The Jews count time from the sun's rising to its setting. So, the sixth hour is about noon. And the sixth to the ninth hour is about noon to three p.m. It was in the middle of the day, yet darkness was all over the land while Christ was suspended on the cross. How could there be such darkness when there was no eclipse of either the Sun or the Moon at that time. Darkness came over all the land when Christ suffered on the cross. It means that the nature witnessed the magnificent suffering of Christ on the cross and suffered together.

It was the most somber moment of history, because humans crucified their Lord. Humans killed the Creator who came into this world to love and to save them. It was the most somber moment in history, because the evil of the world and the power of Satan seemed to overthrow righteousness. And the righteous Son of God found death on the cross as a criminal. It was the darkest moment of human history because the sin of the world and all the burdens that all humans have to bear were laid upon one Man's shoulder. The anguish of humanity fell onto the innocent Lamb of God.

After three hours of darkness, Jesus cried out in a loud voice, "Eloi, Eloi Lama Sabakdani, which means, MY God, My God why you have forsaken me?" The physical pain was enormous, but more sorrowful thing for Him was the emotional distress of being a failure which could have wracked Jesus. He cried out in a loud voice to His Father, wondering if His mission on earth was totally worthless. The deepest and real pain for Christ was His separation from His Father and His feeling of abandonment. Jesus felt that He was abandoned, because He dangled on the cross for three hours without any spiritual aid. No angels appeared. No mighty force of nature crushed His malingerers. However, I feel that by having Jesus hang on the Cross, we are assured that there is always at least one person who can understand us in the time of our own need and in the time of our own despair. And that one person is Jesus. The cry of Jesus on the cross makes us know that when we suffer we do not suffer alone, nor have we been singled out. Our Lord Jesus Christ, the wounded Healer, having been there Himself knows how we feel and how much we hurt. The cry, "why have you forsaken me" was a genuine cry for help in His most excruciating pain. Since the Son of God was also truly human, Jesus was overwhelmed by despair.

When we look at the cross, we can find two aspects of God. First, He is a God of justice. Although Jesus was innocent, now

Jesus was taking upon Himself all the sins of the world. God of justice, therefore, compelled to place a judgment on Jesus. That is why the pain and suffering of Christ was so severe. And now, God even abandoned His Son on the cross.

The other side of God that we can see on the cross is the depth of God's love for humans. God so loved the world that He gave His only begotten Son to save us. God so loved us that He allows Jesus to suffer on the cross.

What happened there on the cross? God's justice and love, two abstractions that hardly coincide, were completed and satisfied in the one body of Christ.

The beautiful music, the prelude of God's victory, was already played as the opening ceremony of redemption history started during Christ our Lord Jesus entered into Jerusalem.

Do you remember the bloody war at the Alamo in Texas when Colonel David Crocket and all his fellow soldiers died? They lost the battle over there in Texas Alamo miserably. However, the history records that because of the sacrifice of the Soldiers at Alamo and the patriotic offering their body for the freedom, the Union of American Soldier won a victory later. Likewise, Christ's suffering and death laid the foundation for the coming victory. It is painful to even hearing Christ's suffering. However, we hear the song of the prelude of the final victory in his entering the city for the suffering.

Christ's Cross as the Hope of Humankind
Matthew 27:45–54, Mark 15:33–41

As I traveled Europe, get into the small village entrance, there were a beautiful sculpture of Christ carved artificially. Some people wear the cross as an accessory.

What does cross mean? What does the cross symbolize? It varies to their view of the Christianity.

The cross is a symbol of hope, although there is also pain. Christ's cross is the hope of the generation because God loves humankind and gave His Son, Jesus, to die on the cross so that we could have eternal life in heaven.

20th centuries ago during the period when the Roman Empire started to conquer the world, there was one Roman soldier, an officer whose regular routine was supervising sentenced criminals' punishment. Seeing the pain of dying on the cross was his routine, it was not a pleasant job yet good pay and respected position in his days. On one Friday during the Passover season of local Jews, it happened for him to witness the severe pain of Jesus Christ during his duty. He wondered why Jesus, Jew, Nazarene man who seemed be a nice person should have gone through such a severe pain. He was a Jew, Jesus of Nazarene, who influenced spiritually and swayed not just His country but also the Greek and Roman world because of His wonderful miracles and the persuasive love for of the people.

On this occasion, it was whole different experience to him. From six in the morning, the other soldiers who worked under his supervision started to nail the man named Jesus on His legs and hands, and they crowned Him with thorns. He saw that Jesus was severely in pain and slowly dying. About noon, he heard that Jesus was screaming loud in extreme pain, "Eloi, Eloi, la ma sabak dani?" which means "My God, my God, why have you forsaken Me?" He heard that Jesus was saying in His last breath, "Father, into your hands I commit my spirit." Then, all of sudden, darkness was cast all over the world even though it was only noon. It was the season of Passover, and it was impossible to have a lunar eclipse. So, this darkness was an unnatural phenomenon. The darkness was not just over the vicinity of their village but overall the world; the sun stopped shining until 6 p.m. So, after approximately twelve hours of Jesus' suffering, the sun gave up its light for six hours.

Andrew Choi

Roman soldier and all the people gathered there, who witnessed Christ suffering on the cross and the darkness came all of sudden should wondered why it became dark when Jesus died on the cross.

Why was there darkness?

First, it was because the master of the universe, the moon, and the sun were dying then.

It was because humankind was killing its master, the creator and sustainer of life and the universe. Christ, along with God the Father, sustains our lives. The Trinity of God makes life in the universe run, and Jesus was dying. So, the sun stopped shining. Not many people knew who Jesus really was. Jesus claimed that He was the Son of God, in essence the very nature of God, and even said the He existed before Abraham, the ancestor of Jewish people. People thought He was crazy. However, He was the Son of God as He claimed, and John testified about Him: "In the beginning was the Word, and the Word was with God, and the Word was God. He was with God in the beginning. Through him, all things were made; without him nothing was made that has been made" (John 1:1–3).

God the Son, Jesus Christ, preexisted and created humankind and the world with God , the Father in the beginning. He made the world even though the world did not recognize Him. People didn't recognize their creator and sustainer and instead caused Him pain, ridiculed Him, and nailed Him on the cross to die. The sun stopped shining and the earth stopped rotating because the creator was dying. There will be a repetition of this catastrophe at the second coming of Christ. Jesus foretold, "The sun will be darkened and the moon will not give its light; the stars will fall from the sky, and the heavenly bodies will be shaken. At that time the sign of the Son of Man will appear in the sky and all the nations of the earth will mourn."

Second, this unnatural phenomenon of darkness is the reflection of the darkness, the sinfulness, of the world. It also was the moment of abandonment and the dark night of the soul because of humankind's sinfulness. It was the moment that God the Father gave up His only begotten Son on the cross because all the sins of humankind were on His shoulders. God had to give up His Son to pay for the all the debt of sins. When Jesus cried, "My God, my God, why have you forsaken Me?" He was not just expressing His deep pain and frustration; God actually had to forsake His Son to pardon humankind's sins. Christ actually went down to hell when there was darkness in the world (1 Peter 3:18–20). Jesus experienced the darkness of the soul.

Forgotten and abandoned!

This mental suffering is more painful than the physical pain that Jesus went through. It was like the deep despair the psalmist went through in Psalm 89:46: "How long, O Lord? Will you hide yourself forever? How long will your wrath burn life a fire?"

Although the cross is so painful, it was the way that God gave us hope.

How this sorrowful and painful event could give humankind a hope?

Frist of all, with his suffering, Jesus was with us all through our pain and suffering. I would like to introduce one amazing testimony of one Jewish boy who went through a horrible experience of hanging.

He testified that "For God's sake, where is God?" And from within me, I heard a voice answer, "Where He is? 'This is where-hanging here from this gallows."[11]

When one Jewish boy, was hung up on a wall at a Holocaust camp, he didn't die—even though the Nazi tried to kill him; his weight was too light. It was more painful not to die, just to hang on. One old lady who looked at his suffering disconsolately stared into the sky and said, "Where is the God of mercy now? Why is God silent now?" Not many could answer that question. Yet one lady, who survived the Holocaust, Corrie Ten-Boon, answered it like this: "I also have no answer to that question. However, I can say that God who came down to the earth and became human suffered, died on the cross, beside the boy [who] suffered." Elie Wiesel who asked, "Where were you God at the dark night of the soul?" also heard the encouraging voice of God in that extreme situation, survived and wrote the noble book Night.

"Never shall I forget the small faces of the children whose bodies I saw transformed into smoke under a silent sky. Never shall I forget those moments that murdered my God and my soul and turned my dreams to ashes. It was then that I understand what had first appealed to me about this young Jew. On that most horrible day, even among all those other bad days, when the child witnessed the hanging of another child who, he tells us, had the face of a sad angel, he heard someone behind him groan. "For God's sake,

---

[11] Elie Wiesel, Night, (New York: Hill and Wang: 1972) (Originally published in 1958 by Les Editions de Minuit, France, as La Nuit), 19–21.

where is God?" And from within me, I heard a voice answer, "Where He is? 'This is where-hanging here from this gallows."[12]

God was there with people who were suffering, and He was agonizing with them. This is hopeful and comforting news.

Second, Christ's dying on the cross there was hope on the cross because it was the day that Christ paid all the debts of humankind's sin; His life was paid as the ransom for the redemption of many. (Mark 10:45)

Hearing Christ's screams of pain, some people ridiculed Him: "Leave Him alone. Let's see if Elijah comes to save Him." However, some people who witnessed Christ suffering and His death on the cross realized that Christ was their Messiah. One centurion and some other Roman guardians, seeing all the events that happened, exclaimed, "Surely, he was the Son of God!" And the criminal who hanged with Christ on the other side rebuked the one who ridiculed Christ, "Don't you fear God? We are punished justly, for we are getting what our deeds deserve. But this man has done nothing wrong." He asked Jesus, "Jesus, remember me when you come into your kingdom." Jesus answered him, "I tell you the truth, today you will be with me in paradise." On the cross, in His extreme pain, Jesus gave hope to the one who was dying without hope and carried him to paradise. Jesus could take this man to paradise because He reconciled him with God through His own death (Mark 10:45). Jesus took all our sins, sorrows, and pains with His ransom; He redeemed us.

Jean Valjean, in the story, *Les Miserables*, was arrested for burglary first then later on became a convict because he attempted to run away from prison. The cold and condemning world made his heart increasingly hardened. People hurt his feelings with their prejudice and unforgiving spirits. He suffered when he was living the difficult life of a prisoner for nineteen years. Even after having been out of jail, a more severe coldness awaited him in the world. Jean Valjean could have easily become angrier and meaner. However, one priest's forgiveness and unconditional love changed him into an honorable man. Jean Valjean became a marvelous Christian. It was the priest who helped him start a new life. To this angry and hateful convict who ran away after stealing the priest's six silver spoon set, the saintly priest gave

---

[12] Elie Wiesel, Night, (New York: Hill and Wang: 1972) (Originally published in 1958 by Les Editions de Minuit, France, as La Nuit), 19-21.

even more valuable things, saying in front of the police who caught him, "I gave you the candlesticks too. They are made of silver like the rest. You can get two hundreds francs for them easily, why didn't you take them with the cutlery?."[13] After the police left, the priest said to Jean, "You no longer belong to evil but to good. It is your soul that I am buying for you. I am taking away from black thoughts and from the spirit of perdition and I am giving it to God.[14] (With these silver candlesticks, I will ransom your soul from anger and hatred. I will buy your soul from the Devil and give your soul back to God.) –Author's paraphrase

---

[13] Victor Hugo, Les Miserables, Fire Side Rockefeller Center (New York: Modern Library Classics A new Translation By Julie Rose, 2009), 89.

[14] Ibid, 90.

Third, the cross is the start of the Christ' resurrection and restoration of human soul.

Two amazing things happened after Christ gave His last breath:

The first thing happed was that the curtain between God and the people was torn down. This event symbolized Jesus breaking the wall between God and us through His body (Hebrews 6:19–20, 9:7– 9, 10:19–21). When Jesus gave Himself as a ransom, He became a mediator and a bridge between God and us, reconciling us with God (Ephesians 2:11–19). This day is more memorable than when the Berlin wall between East and West Germany came down. Jesus could carry a man who was dying hopelessly on the cross to heaven because Jesus reconciled human beings with God. With his cross and the sacrificial death, he started the restoration human soul and reconciliation of human with God, the Father.

Second thing happened was amazing resurrection of the ancient believers : "The tombs broke open and the bodies of many holy people who had died were raised to life. They came out of the tombs, and after Jesus's resurrection they went into the holy city and appeared to many people." (Matthew 27: 51-53).[15]

Think about this unnatural phenomenon. It was not just a local earthquake. It was a global and cosmetic event. Many bodies of saints who died long ago rose. There could be Moses, Elijah, Samuel, and so on. Those people who served God got the guarantee that they would be with God in heaven when they died, yet the promise couldn't be accomplished until Christ paid all the debts of humankind as a ransom. They were like travelers who get a visa to travel to another country yet are not able to get on the airplane. As Christ cut the curtain into two and broke the wall between God and us, those saints who were in a stand-by situation actually could be saved and go to heaven. It was amazing that the sting of death started to get conquered because of the crucifixion of Jesus Christ. Therefore, the resurrection started on the cross and completed when Christ resurrected. There is a saying that "victory starts here." As Jesus died on the cross, victory over the power of death started, and the tombs opened and the saints went into the holy cities.

---

[15] Presentazion di Michelle Prisco, Raffaello, Classici Dell'Arte, Rizzoli Editore Milan, Analisi 18.

That is the hope that Christ gives us on the cross. That was why the Roman officer witnessed during the six hours of darkness could have confessed, "Surely he was the Son of God."

For Reflection and Discussion

1. What did the six hours of darkness when Jesus lay dying on the cross symbolize?
2. Look at the event of Christ on the cross with the eye of the Roman soldier who witnessed. Watch the movie *The Passion of the Christ* and talk about your experience.
3. On the event of Jesus Christ 'crucifixion on the cross and His death, was evil and the darkness overcame the good?
4. What has been your darkest moment of life? Why has Christ's suffering become a comforting message to you?
5. What does *ransom* mean? Why does Christ's suffering on the cross bring hope to you and humankind?
6. Discuss the two amazing things that happened at the moment of Christ's death. How do these events give hope to humankind?

Victory over the power of death as He resurrected

1st Corinthians 15:36-38, 42-44, Luke 24:13-33

Luke described the two young followers of Christ who were despaired after they saw Christ "suffering and death on the cross. On the way to the road of Emmaos, they talked about the things happened when Christ dies on the cross. They were so disappointed and frustrated because they expected Christ would restore the kingdom of Israel and free the Jews from the bondage of Rome's oppression. On the way to Emmaos, Christ who was resurrected approached to them and walked along with them. But they couldn't' recognize Christ.

Listen what they had talked at Luke 24:13-33

Jesus: What are you discussing about as you walk along?

Cleopas: (With amazed look) Are you the only one living in Jerusalem who does'nt know things that have happened in these days?

Jesus: What things?

The follower: About Jesus of Nazareth. He was a prophet, powerful in words and deed before God and all the people, he did so many miracles. So, we hoped that He would restore Israel, but he died on the cross as a criminal. His pain on the cross was horrible and He was so weak and even couldn't resist to the Romans. But the amazing thing was that some of the ladies who followed Christ went to the tomb early this morning and could not find his body. They said that they heard from the angels saying "Christ is alive" Is it possible? They surely had seen the ghost.

(Jesus explained to them from the beginning of Moses books and all the prophets concerning about the resurrection of Christ Himself.)

> Jesus: How foolish you are, and how slow of heart to believe all that the prophets have spoken! Did not the Christ have to suffer these things and then enter His glory?

Resurrection by San Paolo, Museum Dr Arte

Genesis 3:15, Isiah 53, and Joel 2, Psalm 16, and: Psalm 110 prophesied about the Christ's suffering and resurrection. Apostle Peter quoted Psalm 16:8-11as he spoke about Christ resurrection, "God raised Christ from the dead, freeing Him from the agony of death, and because it was impossible for death to keeps its hold on Him. David said about this "I saw the Lord always before me. Because He is at my right hand, I will not be shaken. Therefore my heart is glad and my tongue rejoices. My body also will live in hope, because you will not abandon me to the grave nor will you let your Holy One see decay. You have made known to me the paths of life; you will fill me with joy in your presence." (Acts 2:24-28)

Death is the strongest enemy that nobody could win over, and it has dark shadow, which are fears, sorrows, pain of separation, and sorrow.

If there were no Christ's resurrection and we were not in Christ, death would be our eternal destiny and we all should live under the shadow of death as Apostle Paul said, "Where, O death is your victory? Where O death is your sting? But thanks God, Christ was resurrected and had victory over the power of death. (1st Corinthians 15:55-57)

Flower Blossom from the Root of the Tree

I thought about resurrection and wanted to draw picture of it. The thought comes to me was the, "Spring garden of Keukenhop in Netherland."[16] On the way to visit the spring garden of Keukenhop, I visited the nursery store where they sold seeds. The seeds were tiny; do not have form and no beauty in it. But as they die under the ground and stayed long time under the ground to absorb the nutrition, and take the Sun light, and time passes, it springs up. God gives its own beauty and its own body. As my family visited the garden of Keukenhof, there were amazingly beautiful Lilies, all kinds of flowers with beautiful colors, red, pink, yellow, and purple. 1st Corinthians 15:36-38, 42-44 gives the picture of the resurrection like a spring garden of flowers.

"What you sow does not come to life unless it dies. When you sow, you do not plant the body that it will be, but just for a seed, perhaps of wheat or something else. But God gives a body as He has determined, and to each kind of seed He gives its own body." "So will it be with resurrection of the dead. The body that is sown is perishable, it will be raised imperishable; it is sown in dishonor, it is raised in glory; it is sown in weakness, it is raised in power; it is sown a natural body, it is raised a spiritual body. If there is a natural body, there is also a spiritual body." Paul concludes his resurrection sermon: "So it is written: 'The first man Adam became a living being'; the last Adam, a life-giving spirit. Christ's resurrection gives us hope to live gloriously, happily, eternal life.

---

[16] https://goo.gl/images/wu2gbT

Reconciliation with God and the Restoration of the True Eden: Four Spiritual Principles

Colossians 1:19–20, 2 Corinthians 5:7–8, Revelation 20:1–8, Genesis 1–3

Colossians 1:19–20 says, "For God was pleased to have all his fullness dwell in him, and through him to reconcile to himself all things, whether things on earth or things in heaven, by making peace through his blood, shed on the cross."

There are three themes that can summarize the whole sixty-six books of the Holy Scriptures: the scarlet letter, the thread of love, and the redemption history.

Here is the redemption history that includes the Alpha and the Omega.

1. Garden of Eden: the perfect, happy land
2. The fall of humankind and the predicament: no peace in the human mind, the reality of painful life, and the reign of death
3. God sends Jesus Christ as the reconciler who brings restoration

The Perfect Paradise: Garden of Eden

God had created the perfect, happy place for humankind to live: the garden of Eden. The land had beautiful trees, fruits, happy marriage, abundant food, rivers, and even everlasting life. Most of all, we human beings had no conflicts with God. So, God, after He created the garden of Eden, was so pleased He said, "It is good; it is good." There was no pain, sorrow, suffering, or death. God had created a world in which humankind did not have to suffer. There was happiness, joy, and complete glory.

Let me talk about this happiest place, the garden of Eden, that God originally gave to the human species. We all want happy lives. God gave us all the conditions of happiness in the garden of Eden. Two chapters of Genesis, which are the accounts of creation and the garden of Eden, cover the broad spectrum of the origin of human beings, the beginning of the universe, and human beings' assimilation into life in the garden of Eden. These two chapters of the Bible concern themselves with the principles of a perfect, happy life. The garden of Eden is the original palace where God placed humans, yet humans lost that palace. Someone should have to win back that land. John Milton wrote two important books concerning this topic. One book is entitled *Paradise Lost*, the other book is entitled *Paradise Restored*. These two chapters of Genesis speak about the paradise that was lost. They give us clues of what the paradise restored would look like.

Eden means "delightfulness." So, the garden of Eden means the garden of delightfulness. In Genesis, God has basically two names: the first is Elohim, which means "almighty"; the second name is Jehovah, which means "God of love." In the first chapter, when God creates the heavens and the earth, God's name is Elohim. So, Genesis 1:1 can be read as, "In the beginning the Almighty created the heaven and the earth." Then, in 2:4, God is referred to as Jehovah God. So, it can be read as, "When the Jehovah God [the God of love] made the earth and heavens." He created the garden of happiness. When God created the garden of Eden, God planned for the perfect, happy garden. His love, mighty power, and wisdom made it possible.

Just as good parents want to give their best to their children and prepare happy lives for their children, the Lord Jehovah, who is our heavenly parent, made every condition that made it possible for the achievement of human happiness in the garden of Eden. He also had the ability to make the garden perfectly. So, in the garden of Eden, we can find the glorious condition of happiness.

We find that the ultimate happy life is spiritual life in the garden of Eden. God made human beings spiritual. God formed the first human from dust and gave His Spirit by giving breath through Adam's nostril. At that moment, Adam became a living being. Thus, without spiritual life, there would be no contentment, happiness, or satisfaction in human life. Without spiritual life, people are not living; they are just the dust of the ground. The spirituality of humankind made it possible for us to be connected with God as His children.

The most important condition of a delightful garden was life that lasts forever. In the garden of Eden, there was no death. What were the two important trees in the middle of garden? One was the Tree of Knowledge of Good and Evil. Another was the Tree of Life. The Tree of Life produced fruit that enabled human beings to live forever. To live a long and healthy life is considered to be an important condition of blessedness in every culture and race. Everlasting life is not just a long life; it is a life that has free communion with the living God. Everlasting life was guaranteed in the garden of Eden.

The Human Fall and the Lost Paradise

Everlasting life was guaranteed until Satan invaded and made the human beings hostile with God. Our ancestors Adam and Eve sinned; then suffering and pain intruded on our world. From that time, human beings started to suffer from sin, disease, agony, and sorrow. Most of all, death reigned for all humankind. Satan took away the privilege of "eternal life" that God originally allowed in the garden of Eden, which fatally damaged human beings' happiness.

God exiled the fallen human species from the beautiful garden of Eden. After they were driven out to the east, God placed cherubim and a flaming sword flashing back and forth on the east side of the garden. Why? To guard the way to the Tree of Life so that Adam and Eve could never come back to Eden. To say this differently, the sword of God's judgment stood between the fallen human species and God's garden so that human beings could never return to paradise.

Exiled from the garden of Eden, human beings lost their entire source of happiness and lived instead on the cursed earth. The fall resulted in not only this fatal and damning tragedy for the human race, but it also affected all creation. The universe groaned and suffered the pains of childbirth (Romans 8:21–22). There were hurricanes, tornados, and earthquakes—the cries of the universe—all over the world. This shows God's sense of disharmony, animosity, and unhappiness because of human beings' sinfulness. That is the world we live in even today. We accept it as our predicament and try our best to live better in this confined system.

The Reconciler Jesus Christ and the Restoration

However, the good news is that God started the reconciliation between human beings and Himself through His Son Jesus Christ. Romans 5:12 states, "Just as the result of one man's trespass was the condemnation of all . . ." It is a one-man theory. The Bible is not telling us that only Adam sinned; instead it is telling us that we human beings were all born with original sin because of Adam's original sin. All human beings sin and follow Adam's sinful way of life, since all humankind is from the same root, which is Adam. When people crucified Christ, we all participated in throwing stones at Him, and as a result, we all should suffer the consequences as well.

However, the good news is that humankind's sin, death, and suffering were all pardoned because Christ took all our sins, diseases, and infirmities and became our ransom. With the reconciliation of human beings with God, God brought us a tremendous blessing of restoration. God brought reconciliation and the restored kingdom through Jesus Christ's blood and life; He paid the price of our penalty when He suffered and died on the cross. God promised to give us a new heaven and earth, where human beings could be free from all suffering, pain, and sorrow.

Humankind could be reconciled with God through Jesus Christ and become His loving children because God made Jesus our reconciler; He was able to promise to give us back the perfectly restored Eden, which is the kingdom of God. The most significant thing in the kingdom of God is the absence of death and its power: "And I saw the dead, great and small, standing before the throne, and books were opened. Another book was opened, which is the book of life. The dead were judged according to what they had done as recorded in the books. Then death and Hades were thrown into the lake of fire. The lake of fire is the second death." (Revelation 20:12, 14, NIV), "He will wipe every tear from their eyes. There will be no more death or crying or pain, for the old order of things has passed away." (Revelation 21:4)

> This is the message:
> No more death!
> The power of death is swallowed up by Jesus!
> God promises to give us a new heaven and earth!

The perfectly restored paradise, the kingdom of God, is described in Revelation: "Then I saw a new heaven and a new earth, for the first earth had passed away, and there was no longer any sea . . . He will wipe every tear from their eyes. There will be no more death or mourning or crying or pain, for the old order of things has passed away" (Revelation 21:1, 5).

If someone asked me, "If God is almighty and all knowledgeable and loving, why did He allow Adam to sin and human beings to suffer as the consequence of sin? Can't he stop them from falling?" I have a no good answer for that. I could say that God still loves us, and more importantly, I could say that God turned the sinfulness of human beings to the positive result of the heavenly kingdom. If there were no sin or fall, Adam would only have had the garden of Eden; now human beings can get the privilege of a place much better than the garden of Eden: the kingdom of God, the new heaven and earth.

Restoration

It is a blessing and privilege to get the promise of the restored kingdom of God. To receive that privilege, simply accept Christ the reconciler.

Why don't you open your mind to receive the privilege that God gave us through His Son Jesus Christ?

What would you have to lose? Anxiety, guilt, hell, depression, regrets, emptiness, hopelessness, and death.

What would you have to gain? Everything: heaven, joy, eternal life, a friend, a new life, and hope.

It is such good news, such hope for our generation, so why don't you accept this good news and share it with your friends? Just accept the completed reconciliation and the restoration of God's kingdom and have peace with God! Spread this good tiding. It is beautiful to spread this wonderful news, as Isaiah 52:7 says: "How beautiful on the mountains are the feet of those who bring good news, who proclaim peace, who bring good tidings, who proclaim salvation, who say to Zion, 'Your God reigns!'"

For Reflection and Discussion

1. Do you have your own utopia and happiness? What is your happiness level? What makes you become a happy person? What makes you become a not happy person?
2. What were the conditions of happiness in the garden of Eden, the happy land that God created? Which of those conditions of happiness are we missing now in our lives in the fallen world, the lost paradise? What are humankind's dilemmas after the fall? Could sickness, tragedy, and death, which affect all humankind without exception, be accepted as normal in paradise, the garden of Eden?
3. What is the one-man theory relating to Paul, Adam, and Jesus? What is the hopeful message in the one-man theory? How did God arrange to solve the problems of sin, death, and eternal judgment?
4. Why is Jesus coming as the Savior, the bringer of good news to you and the other people of the world?
5. Think about the day when God will perfectly establish His kingdom. Accept Christ's salvation, and restore the happiness in your life!

CHAPTER 3
HOPE ON THE DAYS OF TRIALS

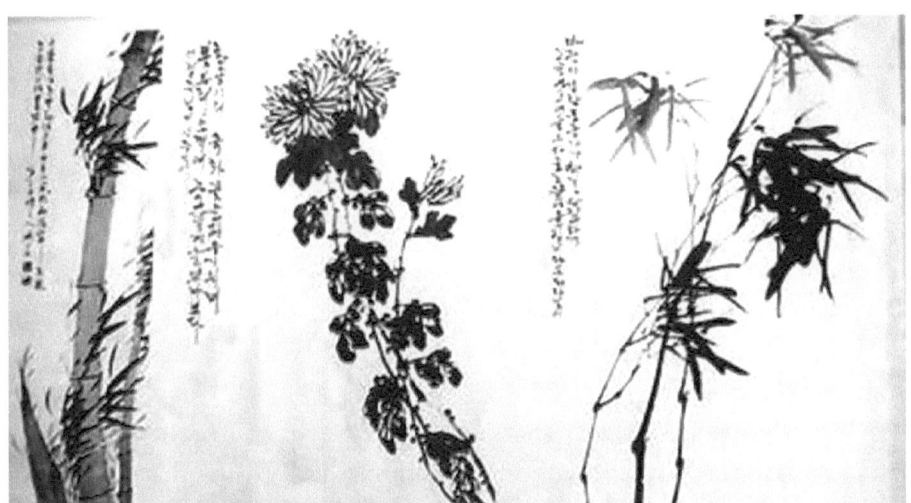

Flower, Gughwach, blossom after enduring the cold winter

Look up to God, who gives you a Positive Perspective and Hope
Job 1:1–22, John 9:1–12

CAN YOU KEEP ON TRUSTING GOD when bad things happen around you, when the pain is sharp and the doubt is deep and it is impossible to see the sense in it all? Yes, we can continue trusting God if we look at things in His perspective.

Life is a continuing response to challenges. The challenges in our lives will be over when our lives end. Some people will fall because they cannot overcome their challenges. However, those who overcome and win their trials will become much stronger and mature people. How you look at a problem determines how you will get through it. The positive perspective that God gives will help you overcome your problems and become victorious. You may start with the same situation as someone else, but the result will be totally different if you look at the problem with God's positive perspective and someone else doesn't.

When someone suffers, what is the response of those who know that suffering is the consequences of sin? They immediately think that something happened to the person because of the person's sin. However, bad things can happen to the good people.

The lives of Job and Joseph in the ancient days teach us about the problem of evil. Jesus also answered to this problem profoundly when His disciples asked, to paraphrase John 9:2, "How was this man born blind? What did he or his parents do wrong?" He defended the man who was born blind: "Neither this man nor his parents sinned,' said Jesus, 'but this happened so that the works of God might be displayed in him'" (John 9:3).

I first want to talk about Job's life to suggest a new perspective on suffering. God defended Job and said He was upright, yet God allowed Satan to attack Job temporarily.

Job lived around 2000 BC and experienced tremendous suffering. He was overwhelmed with sorrow and pain. He was anguished over the burden and hardship of life. His suffering was unbearable, and his pain was beyond his capacity to absorb. Job was afflicted with sores from the bottom of his feet to the top of his head. He took a piece of broken pottery and tried to scrape the sores away. This trial was only a small part of his sufferings. The orthodox theology of that period said that if someone suffers or experiences a disaster, it is because of her sin. God is bringing judgment upon her.

However, this prevailing philosophy is reversed in the book of Job! Throughout the book, our Lord demonstrates a very important truth that not all human suffering is caused by sin.

The book of Job clearly says that Job was *upright* with the Lord and was blameless and shunned evil. In Job chapter one, there is an interesting conversation between God and Satan that illustrates the purity of Job's soul: "Then the Lord said to Satan, 'Have you considered my servant, Job? There is no one on earth like him; he is *blameless and upright*, a man who fears God and shuns evil. And he still maintains his integrity, though you incited me against him to ruin him *without any reason*" (Job 2:3, emphasis added). The Lord said clearly that Job's suffering was given to him not because of his sin but because Satan caused him to suffer. God allowed him to go through trials, but the bottom line is that Job's suffering was not caused by sin. This inspired book radically changed the prevailing theology. It laid the profound theology that even good people could suffer.

Job was the wealthiest, happiest, and most blessed person in the East. God was very proud of Job because of his integrity. Job also was the richest man in those days. In Job Chapter 1 verse 2, it said that "he had 3,000 camels" and that was only one portion of his possessions. In the desert, a camel was very important as it was the best form of transportation. If we compare a camel with a contemporary means of transportation, a camel would be like a Cadillac or a Mercedes-Benz. So, he had 3,000 Benzes, and that was only a part of his possessions.

Trials started to come to Job. Let me refresh your memory with what Job had to endure. Job 1:13–15 reads, "One day when Job's sons and daughters were feasting and drinking wine at the oldest brother's house, a messenger came to Job and said, 'the oxen were plowing and the donkeys were grazing nearby, and the Sabeans attacked and carried them off. They put the servants to the sword, and I am the only one who has escaped to tell you!'"

Job 1:16 reads, "A few seconds later, more bad news came, 'The fire of God fell from the sky and burned up the sheep and the servants, and I am the only one who has escaped to tell you!'"

Job 1:17 reads, "Another messenger came and said, 'The Caldeans formed three raiding parties and swept down on your camels and carried them off. They put the servants to the sword, and I am the only one who has escaped to tell you!'"

Job 1:18 reads, "While he was still speaking, yet another messenger came and said, 'Your sons and daughters were feasting and drinking wine at the oldest brother's house, when suddenly a mighty wind swept in from the desert and struck the four corners of the house. It collapsed on them and they are dead.'"

Finally, all was gone: his family, his possessions, and his health. All that was left was severe suffering.

Natural catastrophe, war, and terror smashed Job's life, and he managed all of those losses. However, when the tragedy came to his loving children, he became angry and expressed his unbearable pain. He tore his robe and shaved his head.

What would you say if you were in that situation? Job immediately fell to the ground and said, "Naked I came from my mother's womb, and naked I will depart. The Lord gave and the Lord has taken away; may the name of the Lord be praised" (Job 1:21).

Still more afflictions befell Job. "Satan went out and inflicted Job with painful sores" (Job 2:7). Job's wife said to him, "Are you still holding on to your integrity? Curse God and die!" (Job 2:9). But Job's response was still a song of loyalty to God: "You are talking like a foolish woman. Shall we accept good from God, and not trouble?"

While sitting on ashes, his head was shaved and his robe was torn. His friends were unable to recognize him. It was an unspeakable moment. Although not many people goes through extreme misery like Job, but we go through similar kinds of problems once in a while in our lives. What would you say about these problems? What perspective would your friends give if you faced these problems?

In Job's situation, his friends came to give their counsel. One of his closest friends, Eliphaz, said, "Job, my good friend, I want to say something to you. I know you are experiencing great stress. I feel pity for you. But I have to tell you this: you are suffering because you have done something wrong" (author's interpretation of Job 4:7–9 and Job chapter 12). Scripture tells that Eliphaz says, "Consider, now: Who, being innocent, has ever perished? Where were the upright ever destroyed? As I have observed, those who plow evil and those who sow trouble reap it. At the breath of God they perish; at the blast of his anger they are no more" (Job 4:7–9). Isn't it cruel to say that? He is not really helping his friend. He is only adding pain to Job's heart.

Now, another close friend of Job's said, "Dominion and awe belong to God; he establishes order in the heights of heaven. Can His forces be numbered? Upon whom does his light not rise? How then can a mortal be righteous before God? How can one born of woman be pure? If even the moon is not bright, and the stars are not pure in his eyes, how much less a mortal, who is but a maggot—a human being, who is only a worm!" (Job 25:2–6).

I think Job's friends wanted to help Job, and their motivation was neither to irritate nor to discourage him. Their advice and wisdom were out of genuine friendship and love. If you look at Job 2:11–13, you will find that genuine love displayed. "They set out from their homes and met together by agreement to go and sympathize with him and comfort him. When they saw him from a distance, they could hardly recognize him; they began to weep aloud, and they tore their robes and sprinkled dust on their heads. Then they sat on the ground with him for seven days and seven nights. During those seven days and seven nights, no one said a word to him, because they saw how great his suffering was."

Their advice and comfort looked so wise and godly. However, it added more pain to Job than the suffering itself. What was the problem? They gave the wrong perspective to this poor suffering man. They applied the wrong theology to this blameless person. They were like physicians who gave the wrong medicine to their patients.

Let's say that there is excellent pain medicine, such as morphine. Morphine works wonderfully well to stop pain. However, if the doctor prescribes morphine to the wrong person, this great medicine would become harmful. Likewise, Job's friend applied the wrong spiritual medicine. His wrong perspective worsened Job's sorrow, and Job became furious. "You smear me with lies; you are worthless physicians, all of you! If only you would be altogether silent! For you that would be wisdom" (Job 13:4–5). They gave Job a negative perspective because they had a misconception about the problem of evil. Sadly, that is what many believers do to their loved ones: penalize, condemn, and put guilt on their loved ones' burned hearts.

However, throughout the book of Job, our Lord demonstrates a very important truth: not all human suffering is caused by sin. Jesus Christ's profound answer to the problem of evil echoes with the theology of Job:

One day, while Jesus was walking on the street in Judea, He saw a man born blind from birth. Here is a paraphrase of the scene: His disciples started to ask, "Why did this tragedy happen to this poor man?" They felt very sorry for the blind man. They wondered, "Why are there always people who have to suffer in this world? Is it because God does not love them, or does God have limited power? Perhaps God just does not care." The disciples arrived to their own conclusion according to the traditional teaching and asked their teacher, Jesus: "Rabbi, who sinned, this man or his parents, that he was born blind?" Their view about the tragedy was exactly like the one that Job's friends held. They firmly believed that when someone experienced pain, it was God's punishment for someone's sin. The rabbis had developed the principle that "there is no death without sin, and there is no suffering without iniquity." They were even capable of thinking that a child could sin in the womb or that its soul might have sinned in a preexistent state. Rabbis also maintained the theory that terrible punishment came to certain people because of their parents' sins.

Let us pause to review their thoughts. Is it really possible that a baby in a mother's womb could commit sin? Is it possible that someone could sin even before he visibly existed and was born into the world?

Although human beings are born with Adam's original sin, children not yet exposed to the temptation of sin are innocent. It is not logical that someone can sin before she is born into the world. Was this man born blind because of his parents' sins? That would not be fair for him. Contrary to the old beliefs, our Lord Jesus adamantly answered His disciples that neither this man nor his parents sinned! It was a simple and short proclamation. However, it was a radical statement in those days. It also was a final word of highest judge.

What a great relief to hear what Jesus said. Nothing is wrong! Jesus explained that the man was born blind so that the work of God might be displayed. Jesus proclaimed that He was the light of the world. To paraphrase,

"I'm the light of the world. As long as it is day, I must do the work of God who sent Me. Night is coming, when no one can work." Jesus had seen this poor man's life through God's perspective. He believed that God had something to do with this man being born blind.

Jesus looked at this man's life positively because He knew that his life was in God's hands.

Jesus looked at the blind man's trial in the light of God.

Jesus believed that God had a purpose for this man and that it was not an accident for him to be born blind.

I am sure that the man who was born blind heard Jesus said positively about his blindness. No doubt he had an overwhelming thought, such as *Wahoo! God's glory and His mighty work will be displayed through me.* Since the man who was born blind accepted Jesus' positive thought, he took the method of Jesus' healing very positively. He did not complain when Jesus put dirt on his eye, and he obeyed when Jesus told him to wash his eye at the pool of Siloam to receive sight.

Let us learn Jesus' positive perspective.

When something goes wrong, our immediate thought is to find someone to blame or to blame ourselves: "What did I do wrong? What did you do wrong?" It could be true sometimes that we did do something wrong and got the result of it. However, even in those cases, God has a plan to make things better and display His wisdom and mighty work and love.

Another of the Old Testament stories that echoes Jesus' positive perspective is that of Joseph. When he was in his teens, his brothers sold him to foreigners as a slave. Well, at one point Joseph was imprisoned, having been caught in a conspiracy and wrongly accused of raping the wife of his lord. Joseph sometimes was starved and suffered great loneliness. He went through lots of suffering. He experienced hardship that wasn't his fault. He was an upright man like Job. If he had looked at his life in a negative way, he would have killed himself or become an angry man bent on revenge.

However, he looked at his life according to the providential will of God and trusted the Lord in every situation. Later on, God blessed Joseph and made him the prime minister of Egypt, which was the strongest nation in those days. He expressed his belief when he was reunited with his brothers. Joseph said to them, "You intended to harm me, but God intended it for good to accomplish what is now being done, the saving of many lives" (Genesis 50:19).

Suffering sometimes could be the consequence of misconduct and sin. However, it is not always the case. Misfortune is not necessarily based on one's sinfulness. As a matter of fact, there are many cases when suffering visits good people. That was especially true in Job's case. Feelings of guilt come when we face trials and troubles in life. However, no longer must we dwell on our guilt because we misunderstand the cause of our suffering. We have to remember that good people also can suffer. Job never lost his sense of hope, although he faced tremendous suffering and was in a seemingly hopeless situation. This was because he believed in the providential will of God and trusted the Lord completely. Job said, "God understands the way to it and he alone knows where it dwells, for he views the ends of the earth and sees everything under the heavens" (Job 28:23–24). God has a purpose for us when we face life's hardships, even though we often do not understand why we are being scourged. However, God does understand, because God knows all things and views the end of suffering. Job said a famous phrase when he was in a great suffering: "After all the trials, I will come forth as gold" (Job 23:10). Taking on God's positive perspective will enable one to be a highly effective person who achieves the highest goals in spite of life's trials.

Job, Joseph, and the man who was born blind and received sight became accomplished people like gold medalists in the Olympics; they glorified God through their trials.

Now, allow me to quote words about attitude from Dr. Norman Vincent Peal on his book, "The Power of Positive Thinking": "Do this with an attitude of faith and you will receive sufficient strength and ability to deal with this problem. Later, if you wish, we can go into analysis of your basic problem."[17]

Harold S. Kushner, Rabbi emeritus, wrote the forward message in the book of Viktor E. Frankl, *Man's Searching for Meaning*: "Forces beyond your control can take away everything you possess except one thing, your freedom to choose how you will respond to the situation. You cannot control what

---

[17] Norman Vincent Peale, The Power of Positive Thinking, (New York, Ballantine Books, 1952), 110.

happens to you in life, but you can always control what you will feel and do about what happens to you."[18]

We can either choose to become morose, staggered by the weight of the trial and consider the bitter taste of that trial like the sour taste of a lemon or we can choose to deal with that trial with a positive attitude and make that lemon into lemonade.

People who are in bad heath, having financial difficulties, or struggling in their marriages lose hope not just because of their difficult situations but because they think negatively. As believers and followers of Christ, we should think like Christ and be positive in any situation. We should look at our lives in the light of God's good providential will.

At this time, I want to encourage you to look at the problems you and others face with God's positive perspective. I've seen so many people's lives become more miserable and hurt not because of what they had faced but because of their friends' negative comments and, most of all, their negative perspective on their lives. Get a new perspective through Jesus. Believe in God's love and His good will for your life. Develop a deep faith in God that will give you faith in yourself. I pray for you to look at God, who is the ultimate good, who would bring good even out of evil. Keep on trusting God even through hardship. May God give you a positive perspective, bless you, and shine upon your life, that you would become happy and victorious even in times of trouble.

For Reflection and Discussion

1. If God is almighty and loving, then could God allow bad things to happen in a good person's life? Is God not good? Is the power of evil stronger than God?
2. Talk about the problem of evil in our lives. What do you think about the nine-year-old pure and lovely girl who died in January 2011 because of some gunmen's crazy shooting in Arizona?
3. What would you say if you were in Job's situation in Job 1? Read what Job said at that moment (Job 1:21).

---

[18] Viktor E. Frankl, Man's Searching for Meaning, (Boston, MA: Wilsted & Taylor Publishing Services, 1959), 8.

4. What were Job's friends' misunderstandings about the problem of evil? How do their misunderstandings distort God's nature and hurt the people who are suffering?
5. How did Joseph overcome the overwhelming sorrow and tragedy of his life? What was Joseph's view on the tragedy that he had experienced because of his stepbrothers selling him as a slave?
6. Meditate on what Jesus said: "neither the parents nor their blind son did anything wrong." Nothing wrong! Jesus continued: "But this happened so that the work of God might be displayed through the suffering of this born-blind man's life" (John 9:3–5, author's paraphrase). How does Jesus' statement give hope to you and to others who are suffering?

Look up to God, Who Disciplines and Refines You Like Gold in Times of Suffering
Hebrews 12: 5–13, 1 Peter 5:5–7, Job 23:10

Hebrews 12:5–6 says that God expresses His love toward us by discipline: "And you have forgotten that word of encouragement that addresses as sons: 'My son, do not make light of the Lord's discipline, and do not lose heart when he rebukes you, because the Lord disciplines those he loves, and he punishes everyone he accepts as a son.'"

Let me first tell you what this Scripture does not mean. God's original intent is not to cause His children to suffer. Instead of suffering and pain, He wants to protect His children from any harm and bless them in many ways. God wants to give good lives to His children. God's plan for our lives is not to destroy us but to give us great futures with prosperity and abundant life: "'For I know the plans I have for you,' declares the Lord, 'plans to prosper you and not to harm you, plans to give you hope and a future'" (Jeremiah 29:10–11).

However, there will be occasions when we can not avoid suffering; God will allow it. The world we live now is not a perfect place; the Devil still plays a big part in this world's operation. Even Jesus said that we would suffer tribulations.

First of all, suffering promotes us to become mature and builds up our characters.

Paul said to the Romans, "And we boast in the hope of the glory of God. Not only so, *but we also glory in our sufferings, because we know that suffering produces perseverance; perseverance, character;* and character, hope. And hope does not put us to shame, because God's love has been poured out into our hearts through the Holy Spirit, who has been given to us" (Romans 5:2b–5, emphasis added). Our character is the "harvest of righteousness and peace" mentioned in Hebrews 12:11: "No discipline seems pleasant at the time, but painful. Later on, however, it produces a harvest of righteousness and peace for those who have been trained by it."

Suffering is not pleasant; rather, it is painful. However, it produces a harvest, forms a mature and understanding character, and refines us. That is our hope in times of suffering.

As I watched the Olympic athletes' performances, I was amazed by their beautiful artistry. It was amazing, but it was just the tip of the iceberg of their hard training, which required a lot of sweat and continuous effort. It was the result of their pain. Their beautiful performances are the harvest of the suffering. The winter 2009 Olympic figure skating gold medalist, Kim Yu Na, performed amazingly—artistic and beautifully. Not many people knew that she and her parents spent many tearful years of training to reach that level. As Job said, after trials, we "come forth as gold" (Job 23:10).

No pain, no gain!

No trials, no noble characters!

The great men and women in the Bible and in human history prove that character counts. David, Job, Joseph, Daniel, Moses, Abraham Lincoln, and countless other great people of history have proven this truth. Therefore, when you are discouraged in times of suffering and trials, look to the future with the hope that you will come out as refined gold. Rejoice in times of suffering by looking forward to the moment when you will stand at the podium to get God's gold medal.

God approves and loves those who overcome adversity and trials and become successful.

God will form you as a humble servant leader through suffering.

God wants His servants to become humble. Suffering and trials form you to become humble. That is what Peter says in 1 Peter 5:5–7: "Young men, in the same way be submissive to those who are older. All of you, clothe yourselves with humility toward one another, because God opposes the proud, but gives grace to the humble. Humble yourselves, therefore under God's mighty hand, that he may lift you up in due time. Cast away your anxiety on him because he cares for you."

Moses and David are good examples of those who became humble servants because of the discipline and trials they went through.

Moses, when he was young adult, was a patriot and had zeal for justice, yet he was never described as humble.

Moses' humbleness reached all over the face of the earth when he led the Israelites. Humbleness became his nature later; it flowed out of him from his everyday life naturally in his leadership. It was who he was. It took several decades for him to become a humble leader. There is an oriental saying: "When a decade passes, even the nature of the mountain and the river will change." That is required; no genius forms overnight. God spends a long time forming one person's character. I sometimes wonder why God is not so quick to use His servants; I have asked, "Why wait so long? Why does God waste His time and a person's life?" Because He knows that character counts: one leader can change the course of history and affect the lives of so many people.

Moses was in a high and noble position, the prince who could become the next king of Egypt, which was the strongest country of those days. He was highly trained and educated, and he was a strong man. He did not realize that he was arrogant and naughty then. God cast him out to the wilderness and had him spend forty years of his life as a shepherd in a foreign country. He spent his lonely and hard life there. His agony living in a foreign country was well expressed when he named his son Gershom, which means, "I have become an alien in a foreign land" (Exodus 2:22).

Saul's is another story of one who spent his painful life to harvest a humble character. God first chose Saul as a leader because he was a humble man, yet Saul became an arrogant king. God took him off the throne and chose David as the next king. David had the potential to become a humble man. God allowed him to experience trials and disciplined him so that he would form a character of humbleness. God anointed him when he was young, even before he fought and beat the giant, Goliath. Even after God had anointed him, it took a decade for him to become anointed as a real king at Hebron. After that, it still took eight more years for him to become the king of Israel at Jerusalem. During those eight years, he lived a hard life in the mountain dungeon because Saul chased after him to kill him. During those trials, David expressed his agony, saying, "I am like a dead dog." He felt bad and depressed many times. However, God allowed him to suffer in order to refine and carve the diamond character of humility inside him. The proverb said, "Iron sharpens iron" (Proverbs 27:17). I remember the days of my twenties when I felt so much pain because God was molding me as a humble person.. People say the twenties are beautiful, yet not for me; there were miserable days of humiliation and trials. I also remember the days when I was young captain, a junior Chaplain in Brussels Europe; felt sharp pain when God molded me as his humble servant. However, I realize now that those sharp irons formed me into who I am now.

If you feel pity for yourself because of the suffering you face, look up to God, who gives you the opportunity to become a humble servant leader!

Second, suffering helps you become a more understanding person; as a result, you become a good comforter to those who go through the same kind of suffering.

King David had gone through so much suffering. His experiences of suffering and various trials made him able to become a man of understanding and a real comforter. Many who had experienced hardship in their lives were able to gather around David because he was not just a boss to them but a friend; he was a comforter who understood their pain. He was like a magnet that pulls and draws others. David put his experience of suffering as a big highlighted letter when he wrote his resume as a leader. Likewise, you can put your experience of suffering on your résumé and highlight it: "I went through it. Been there, done that, understand you."

Suffering is on Jesus' résumé, as it was in Hebrews 4:14–16, "Therefore, since we have a great high priest who has ascended into heavens, Jesus the Son of God, let us hold firmly to the faith we profess. For we do not have a high priest who is unable to empathize with our weaknesses, but we have one who has been tempted in every way, just as we are—yet he did not sin. Let us then approach God's throne of grace with confidence, so that we may receive mercy and find grace to help us in our time of need." Jesus is our real comforter and wounded healer because He went through trials and suffered. Isaiah 53:3, 5 says, "He was despised and rejected by mankind, a man of suffering, and familiar with pain. But he was pierced for our transgressions, he was crushed for our iniquities; the punishment that brought us peace was on him, and by his wounds we are healed."

When you experience great trials, you may want to ask, "Do you know what I am saying, and can you understand what I am going through?" Jesus will say, "My son, daughter, I've been there, I've been gone through same like you," and He will put His arm around you and say, "I truly understand you; I am with you."

If you have a painful memory of your childhood or youth that you want to erase, you have two choices; one is to hold a grudge and be angry about the bad memories; another is to become a more understanding person. When you choose to become positive, your painful experience will help you become a good counselor and comforter to those who go through the same trouble that you experienced. Joyce Myer shared the experience of her painful childhood. She said that she became a real comforter and minister to those in trouble because she had gone through similar suffering. She said, "I know exactly what you are going through now, and God will understand you truly and will comfort you."[19] (author's paraphrase)

Paul said in the 2 Corinthians 1:3–7,

Praise be to the God and Father of our Lord Jesus Christ, the Father of compassion and the God of all comfort, who comforts us in all our troubles, so that we can comfort those in any trouble with the comfort we ourselves receive from God. For just as we share abundantly in the sufferings of Christ, so also our comfort abounds through Christ. If we are distressed, it is for your comfort and salvation; if we are comforted, it is for your comfort, which produces in you patient endurance of the same sufferings we suffer. And our hope for you is firm, because we know that just as you share in our sufferings, so also you share in our comfort.

Jesus weeps with you when your spirit mourns. It was the same with Paul when he wrote the letter to the Corinthians (2 Corinthians 1:3–7).

If you are weary with the burden of life, do not fall into self- pity or complain. Look up to God, who refines your character into humbleness. It is the opportunity that God refines you like a pure diamond. Look at this as an opportunity for God to form you into a more understanding person who could become a real comforter for others.

Blessed are those who overcome difficulties and become real victors, who possess the humble, servant leader's character and who could comfort others. God will approve of those people's lives as the lives of real victors. God will be sure that they live blessed and beautiful lives.

For Reflection and Discussion

1. Is God's original intent to bless you to have an abundant and happy life or to cause you to suffer? Then, why does God allow suffering?

---

[19] Joyce Meyer, Seven Things that Steal Your Joy, (New York: Warner Books, 2004), 195.

2. What is the purpose of God allowing you to suffer and be disciplined? How could suffering be a means to achieve God's will in your live and make your life better?
3. Talk about the good characters that God built in the lives of Moses, David, and Joseph when they struggled in times of suffering.
4. Talk about those whom you respect most who have experienced hardship and how their hardship has helped form their good characters. You can talk about your own life experiences too.
5. Meditate on 2 Corinthians 1:3–7 and Hebrews 4:14–16 and think about how God formed Paul as a person of understanding who could comfort others.
6. Meditate on Isaiah 53:1–5 and think about Jesus, the wounded healer and real comforter.

Look up to Jesus When Strong Storms Blow into Your Life

Trial and Victory
Matthew 14:22–33, Psalm 107:23–30

This Scripture is about Jesus calming the storm and Peter walking on water. The success of the Scripture lesson can be measured by the success of its application. So, after reading this lesson, I want all of you to walk on water. Then, I will know that God approves of this lesson.

Today's story tells us four encouraging truths.

1. **Jesus, who is the same yesterday, today, and tomorrow, is praying for you.**

When the storm blows strongly against you, not only holding you in the same place and keeping you from moving even an inch but pushing you away from your purposes, your goals, and your destination, what will you feel?

Frustration Agony Anger Sadness Hopelessness Panic

Now, the disciples of Jesus were experiencing those kinds of hardship (Matthew 14:22–24). The boat that the disciples rode on had already gone a considerable distance from the land. It seemed like there was no hope of going back to where they came from. It was too late. The situation already had been developed too far. The boat was buffeted by the waves. That was the reality they faced. They were looking for solutions, yet nothing seemed to work. They had no other option but to sink down into the water. So, they felt hopeless, helpless.

Of course, you would be frustrated, agonized, and if the situation lasted longer than your ability could endure, then you would also be exhausted, fatigued.

There are ups and downs in life for all of us, and we can't predict when there will be downs. Some of you may now be experiencing the strong wind against your life and breaking the peace of your life's journey. For some of you, the storm may already have passed; you might laugh about it as you remember those days. All of us experience strong storms blowing against us.

However, the good news is that while the disciples were fighting against the wind, feeling discouraged and hopeless, Christ the Lord was praying for them in the mountain. You may say, "Pray later, Lord! Now come to rescue me!" But, to Jesus, praying was the priority because it was the source for drawing God's help to our lives. Although the disciples couldn't see Him or even think about His reasoning, Jesus' praying for them was the source of their power and protection from the storm.

Even when nobody seems to care about you, when it seems there is no solution, we still have hope because our Lord Jesus Christ is praying for us at the right hand of God's throne in heaven. Jesus Christ cares about you and remembers you and prays for you in your time of adversity. Even when we do not know what we ought to pray, even at the moment when we want to give up, the Spirit of God will intercede for us and pray for us with unspeakable words: "Likewise the Spirit also helped our infirmities: for we know not what we should pray for as we ought: but the Spirit itself makes intercession for us with groaning which cannot be uttered" (Romans 8:26).

Jesus' prayer was the intercessory prayer. It was the prayer of Moses and Paul. It was the prayer of the mother of Augustine who prayed many years for her prodigal son.

So, remember that you are not forgotten; remember that Jesus is praying in heaven. Jesus Christ, who is same yesterday, today, and tomorrow, is praying for you in heaven now.

Mighty God, the Son, is praying for you. We can look up to Him as the psalmist said: "I lift up my eyes to the hills—where does my help come from? My help comes from the Lord, the maker of heaven and earth. He will not let your foot slip—he who watches over you will not slumber; indeed, he who watches over Israel will neither slumber nor sleep. The Lord watches over you—the Lord is your shade at your right hand; the sun will not harm you by day, nor the moon by night" (Psalm 121:1–6).

Jesus Will Approach You to Rescue You

Even if we have no strength to hold onto hope, Jesus Himself will come to hold you up and rescue you! When He comes to you, nothing can interrupt Him!

As we read in Matthew chapter 14 verse 25, it was "the fourth watch," which means that it was between 3 a.m. and 6 a.m. Jesus approached His disciples shortly before dawn, when they were still fighting against the wind. The disciples had departed from the land the previous evening. So they had been struggling with the strong wind all night, for approximately twelve hours. They should have been exhausted. At that moment, they saw a vague human figure in the mist, walking on the water and slowly approaching them. It was their Lord, Christ. When the disciples saw Christ, they thought He was a ghost. They were terrified. They cried out with fear and said, "It is a ghost."

When we are exhausted, even our helper looks like a ghost. But remember that Christ, our helper and rescuer, approaches us to rescue and lift us up. More importantly, when Jesus walks toward you, nothing will interrupt Him. The waves of the sea, the storms, and the outraged waters couldn't interrupt Jesus' coming to His disciples.

Therefore, there is nothing that can separate us from the love of God in Christ Jesus our Lord. Romans 8:37–39 says, "No, in all these things we are more than conquerors through him who loved us. For I am convinced that neither death nor life, neither angels nor demons, neither the present nor the future, nor any powers, neither height nor depth, nor anything else in all creation, will be able to separate us from the love of God that is in Christ Jesus our Lord."

Why do nations rage against each other? The kings of the earth rise up, and the rulers ban together against the Lord. Is God living and still sovereign? Yes, the Lord reigns and rescues us.

Jesus Will Give You Courage to Walk on Water

Jesus, who was walking on water, said to His frightened disciples, "Take courage! It is I! Do not be afraid."

In war, we have two enemies: one is our literal enemy, and the other is our fear. The stronger enemy is fear. If we have the courage to overcome our fear, we can calm the situation and overcome the storms. If we look at Him instead of at the outraged waters and situation, Jesus will give us courage. Since our Lord is the one who walks on water, why should we worry about the storm? All we have to do is trust Him and walk with Christ like Peter.

When Jesus said, "It is I; do not be afraid," Peter replied, "Lord, if it is you, tell me to come to you on the water." He wanted to walk on water with Christ. Amazingly, he walked on water. But later he started to sink because he focused on the wind, not Jesus.

Does anyone want to walk on water?

If I had been in Peter's position when Jesus asked him if he wanted to walk on water, I might have responded, "Sir, I will pass it to James, Matthew, or Thomas." Thomas would have said, "Peter, you'd better first give me proof that you can walk on water." Once in a while in our lives, we need to walk on water.

Life has ups and downs. However, I can share one important secret of how to live a successful and victorious life in any situation:

When we focus on Jesus in the midst of our difficulty and have the courage to face the difficulty, challenge it, and overcome it, we will walk on water no matter what situation we are in. However, when we focus on the wind, only concentrating on the negative situation, we will sink! I can tell this truth based on Scripture and my own experiences. What you believe is more important than your circumstances.

Take Courage

Life does not guarantee us that we will always have rosy days. We sometimes have to face financial problems, nagging health, and marriage struggles. Even Jesus doesn't guarantee us that we will always have easy days. Instead, Jesus makes us aware that we will have tribulation while we live on this earth. However, Jesus promises that if we have courage to fight against our enemies, fear and discouragement, we shall have victory. Jesus said, "You will have tribulation in this world. However, take courage because I have overcome evil." If you worry, feel discouraged, or are depressed, I want to challenge you with what Jesus says today: "Take courage, Jesus loves you! Jesus is with you. Do not be afraid."

Winston Churchill, former prime minister of the United Kingdom, gave a famous speech to his people when they were afraid and panicking in the middle of World War II: "Do not give up, and take courage! Do not give up! Do not give up! Take courage!"

Invite Christ into your life as navigator and captain of your life, and the Lord will calm the storm.

"Some went out on the sea in ships; they were merchants on the mighty waters. They saw the works of the Lord, his wonderful deeds in the deep. For he spoke and stirred up a tempest that lifted high the waves. They mounted up to the heavens and went down to the depths; in their peril their courage melted away. They reeled and staggered like drunkards; they were at their wits' end. Then they cried out to the Lord in their trouble, and he brought them out of their distress. He stilled the storm to a whisper; the waves of the sea were hushed. They were glad when it grew calm, and he guided them to their desired haven." (Psalm 107:23–30)

If you have courage and consistently believe that you will overcome, you will not fail. God will give you serenity in your heart and calm the situation as Jesus calmed the storm at Galilee. So it is my prayer for you today that God will give you courage and calmness and help you walk on water even on stormy days. Amen.

For Reflection and Discussion

1. Was there a moment in your life when a storm was striking you? What was your response?
2. Meditate on Psalm 121:1–6, and visualize Christ praying for you now.
3. Experience calmness in your mind.
4. Meditate on Romans 8:37–39; visualize and trust Christ, who is intervening in your life to rescue you from any dangers.
5. What is the secret to overcoming adversity and becoming a victor? Are you looking at Jesus or just looking at the wages of storms? Are you a conqueror or a victim of your circumstances?
6. Look to Jesus, who calms the storm, and walk with Him on water.

Invite Jesus to be the captain of your life, and experience the victory, tremendous serenity, and calmness He brings.

Be hopeful and Focus on the future goal
Philippians 3:12-21

This letter that Paul addressed to the Philippians will be a very meaningful message for us today in our first worship service of the year. A new year is always exciting because it allows us to dream anew and to set new goals. Today's passage tells us three things for us to start hopeful life. I want to challenge you with Paul's message to the Philippians to get a new feeling, to breathe the new air of the New Year.
1. We should have a goal for this year.
2. We should have a humble attitude.
3. We should look forward to the future.

I. Toward the goal of life

Do you have a goal for this year or are you just going to live an extension of last year? Are you still living in the past? To succeed in life, we must first set up our goal. Today is the first day of the rest of our life. Apostle Paul exhorts us to 'press toward the goal to win the prize'. No doubt Paul is one of the greatest figures in Christian history who lived successfully in the history. Why was he successful? He was successful because he had a goal. When Paul wrote the Philippians Epistle, he was already a matured old man. His spiritual son Timothy was grown up and became a pastor of his own flock. Furthermore, Paul was in prison and faced a trial that could end up the life as a criminal. Think about it- Paul was in prison when he said 'I have a goal for my life'. If Paul in his situation could have a goal for his life, how much more could we, who are free, have a goal? Someone might say, "Setting a goal! I had done many times. It just makes me frustrated because I realized that I failed to accomplish every year." However, making a goal motivates you to try again and it gives purpose of your life.

II. Humble atttitude of life

Apostle Paul had the gray hair that showed his wisdom. He was a matured and well-knowledgeable Christian when he said in verse 12, 'I do not say that I have at this time grasped the meaning of Christ, or that I have already become perfect in my knowledge of Him. But I keep pressing on to apprehend Christ Jesus.'

As you already know, Paul wrote most of the epistle in the New Testament- over half of the New Testament. He is the one who established the ground of Christian Faith andTheology, yet he said, 'I indeed apprehended him not'. He should be the one who could say 'I fully apprehend Christ'. Yet he realized that he had not grasped the meaning of Christ and he said, 'I had not fully apprehend and need to grow more'. It was a humble and honest confession of the old man. That was why he still had room to grow and he still had hope for the future. He still had excitement for the dream that he was awaiting. He still enjoyed learning. All this is summed up in his statement, 'I do not say that I have at this time grasped the meaning of Christ'. This is the final words of the greatest Christian who ever lived, spoken in the face of death concerning his unquenchable spiritual desire to learn more about Christ. This desire is seen in the words of the song 'More About Jesus'. Listen to the words:

More about Jesus let me learn

More, more about Jesus More of His saving fullness

See more of His love who died for me.

III. Forget what is behind and look forward to the future

To live this New Year successfully, we first need to forget what is behind and look forward to the future. We need to look ahead and not dwell in the past. We have a tendency to remember what we have to forget and forget what we have to remember. Paul's attitude leads us to success because He could say that 'to forget what is behind and stretch out to what lies before'. Regretting could be the opportunity to see you in the past mirror. But if we let regret fills us with remorse and it would limit our ability of do new things in the future. Then, we are not living in the present time. We cannot relive the past. So, just learn the lessons and use the past as a mirror and tell your junior how to have a better life with lessons you've learned from the past failure. Most of all, we should live in the present time and look forward to the future.

Paul said in verse 16, "In any case, let us live up to whatever truth we have already attained'.(NIV) New King James Version make me to understand this verse more clearly, "To the degree that he have already attained, let us walk by the same rule." Either failure or success, we Christians should live up to whatever we have already attained. The reality of the present situation, whatever it is, is always the starting point and the ground that we can stand upon. We can't do anything about the past days- we can't correct, change, and add to those things already happened. But the future, which is before us, is a field of possibility that we can create a new history.

To look forward to the future, we need to look everything in God's perspective.

God, as the One who sovereigns our life, has intervened in our lives and has led us to the present situation in whatever areas of your life; marriage, career, family, location, and friendship. We have to trust that God is the one who leads our life to the present time and unto this situation.

Because Paul acknowledged the divine guidance for him, he could release him from the past and look toward the future and could press forward to the goal. He says, "I press on toward the goal". Another translation of this verse is, "I keep running toward the goal marker, straight for the prize to which God called me to get the prize that is contained in Christ Jesus." The Sun of this New Year rose already. With the great expectation, hope, excitement, and freshness, let us run the track of this New Year. Take off all the burden of regret or pride of old year. Let us allow God to release our souls from the past failure and hurt and regrets, work on your new days, and look up to the prize that is stored in heaven.

COMMIT THY WAY TO THE LORD
Psalm 37: 1-7

In Psalm 37: 3-7, there are important principles that we can apply when we make decisions for life. Let us listen to these words pray- fully, "Trust in the Lord and do good; dwell in the land and enjoy safe pasture. Delight yourself in the Lord and He will give you the desires of your heart. Commit your way to the Lord; trust on Him and He will do this: He will make your righteousness shine like the dawn, justice like the noonday sun. Be still before the Lord and wait patiently for Him." This Psalm gives principles of life.

Life in essence is in a changing mode all the time. So, we ask for change at the coming New Year. This request for change requires us to choose which way to go and therefore life is choosing. When we go to the market to buy something with a certain amount of money, we have to choose between items. Sometimes we do not make wise choices; sometimes we are pleased with our choices. If choices are required a small grocery, those choices are not grave. But if it is a decision about choosing career, a school, and a marriage, in a rare case big decision to choose the national diplomacy direction, it is not always easy. This Bible principle from Psalm 37, commit thy way to the Lord, gives a solid foundation to get the wise and hopeful decision of choosing the right way.

First Principle: Do Good, Then, You will dwell in the Land and get blessing to enjoy a safe pasture.

Sometimes we wonder why the other people, who were not honest before God and commit wrong actions prosper more than the person, who is sincere and honest. This bothered the Psalmist so much and it was expressed in verses 1-2. Psalm 10: 1-5 also said, "Why, O Lord, do you stand far off? Why do you hide yourself in times of trouble?" In his arrogance the wicked man hunts down the weak, which are caught in the schemes he devises. He boasts of the craving of his heart; he blesses the greedy and reviles the Lord. In his pride the wicked does not seek God; in all his thoughts there is no room for God. But his ways are always prosperous." When we look at the unfairness and injustice, we are discouraged. These injustices discourage us continue to do good acts. However, if we realize that God's goodness rewards those who do good deed and trust Him, we can continue to do good act. Psalmist says that 'I am going to continue to do good deeds and I am always happy.' Psalmist recommends us "Trust in the Lord and do good; dwell in the land and enjoy safe pasture." Remember always that God is the one who sovereigns the world with His goodness. That guarantees our safety and insures an enjoyable life. The life of the man of Faith says that eventually the person who did good get the amazing rewards from God who is the source of blessing. As an example, I want to tell you about the life of Enoch. In Hebrew, it said, "Enoch was commended as one who pleased God." In his lifetime, Enoch had so much suffering; he hardly received any recognition, instead he experienced much persecution. However, God recognized Enoch and commended him as one who pleased God and took Enoch to heaven. Enoch did not even experience the pain of death when he was about to depart this world. So, the author of Hebrews recommends having faith like this, "Without faith, it is impossible to please God, because anyone who comes to Him must believe that He exists and the He rewards those who honestly seek Him." (Hebrews 11: 6) Our God, who is good exists and reins the world and history. He rewards those who do good deed.

Rewards come in many ways. God could reward us with material blessings, but it is not always materialized. It could be inward affirmation first; however, His rewards are greater than any other rewards. Remember what the Lord said to Abraham in Genesis 15: 1 "Do not be afraid, Abram, I am your shield, your great reward." As we prepare for the upcoming year, I want to remind you that God is good, so it is a great wisdom to do good acts. One of the ways to do good is plant good seed of Gospel, live as a good Samaritan to your neighbor. You may not get the benefit right away, yet God who is good surely gives you the eternal rewards. The wisdom word said, "Cast your bread upon the waters, for many days you will find it again." When we do good deed in this world, it seems like we are throwing bread into the water just to see the bread sink. But someday, you will find your bread. When you bless others, that blessing will return to you. When he blesses open the floodgates of heaven and pour out so much blessing, it will be amazingly abundant." (Malachi 3: 10)

Second Principle: Delight yourself in the Lord and believe that your hope and wishes would come true.

Most assuredly, God will give you the desires of your heart. Every human being has desires in their heart. We all human have every right to pursue happiness. I am certain that as we start this New Year we all are making fine wishes for the New Year. Christian faith supports those good wishes; of course, if those desires do not offend God's will or the desires aren't from ones greediness. As we sing, I do wish that you and your families have a very Happy New Year and that all of you to achieve the desires of your heart in the New Year. Just delight in the Lord and God will satisfy the desire of your heart. (verse 4)

Third Principle: Commit your way to the Lord

Commit your way to the Lord and Trust in Him and He will make your righteousness shine like the dawn, and the justice of your will shall make you like the noonday sun. Wisdom word says, "Trust in the Lord with all your heart and lean not on your own understanding; in all your ways acknowledge him, and he will make your paths straight."(Proverbs 3:5-7)

Like sheep, we always need the shepherd's guide. We want to know which direction is toward peace and abundant life. In order to make good choice, we use our knowledge, experience, and our understanding. However, sometimes it is not easy to acknowledge which direction is the best way for achieving peace and life. In those conflicting times, we must continue to trust in the Lord, lean on Him and commit our direction to the Lord. In other words, we must acknowledge God' presence and the guide in all things.

Nothing in our life happens as an accident. You encounter people and experience some events because God plan for you with good intention. Be mindful of God's presence and follow the path that Jesus would lead you. Romans 11:33 says, "Oh, the depth of the riches of the wisdom and knowledge of God; How unsearchable His judgments and His paths beyond tracing out"

The encouraging word is in Psalm 37 verses 23, 24: "If the Lord delights in your way, he makes his steps firm; though he stumble, he will not fall, for the Lord upholds him with his hand." Who would fall if the strong and might Lord's hand uphold? Who would astray if God lead with His unsearchable wisdom?

Fourth Principle: Be still before the Lord

Sometimes, we couldn't do anything about the situation. At that time, all we could do is still in the Lord and waiting patiently. On those days, just be still before the Lord. Just step back and watch what the Lord is doing. If the Lord delights in your way, He makes your steps firm. If the Lord delights in your way, you will not fall even though you may stumble, because the Lord upholds you with His mighty and graceful Hand. Reinhold Niebuhr prayed in his famous serenity prayer that: "God! Grant me the serenity to accept the things I cannot change; courage to change the things I can; and wisdom to know the difference."

It is my prayer for you to be ready for the great New Year! Give your good wishes to the Lord. Live a new life. Do good deed. Commit thy way to the Lord and be still in the Lord. Then, God will bless you make your life righteous and shine like the dawn in the morning and the noonday light.

Summary:
Key verses:

> "Trust in the Lord and do good; dwell in the land and enjoy safe pasture. Delight yourself in the Lord and He will give you the desires of your heart. Commit your way to the Lord; trust on Him and He will do this: He will make your righteousness shine like the dawn, justice like the noonday sun. Be still before the Lord and wait patiently for Him."

➢ Conditional blessing: If you do this, then

One condition: Trust

Pairing concept Scriptures in the New Testament is Philippians 4: 6 "Do not be anxious about anything, but in everything, by prayer and petition, with thanksgiving, present your request to God.

Then, Blessing of Peace will be in your heart and minds. (Philippians 4:7)
- ✓ Trust
- ✓ Do Good
- ✓ Commit your way to
- ✓ Be Still

What does it mean "Trust in the Lord"?
What does it mean "Commit Thy way to the Lord"?

➤ Then, Blessings comes in the New Year 2019:

- ✓ Verse 3: Dwell in the land and enjoy safe pasture
- ✓ Verse 6: Your righteousness shines like the dawn, justice like the noonday sun.
- ✓ Psalm 37 verses 23, 24: "If the Lord delights in your way, he makes his steps firm; though he stumbles, he will not fall, for the Lord upholds him with his hand."

Ebenezer: Thus Far the Lord has helped Us
1st Samuel 7:12-1, Exodus chapter 14-15

As I prepare the sermon for today, the last Sunday of 2018, I thought about what is the best way to conclude the yr. 12, and welcome the 2019 the New Year.

First of all, remember what God has done good things in my life and give thanks

Second, if there is something that is not resolved, not settled, or if there is something that you feel it as your failure that lead you to feel sad and pitiful, i) Look into the problems in God's positive point of view, Give it to the Lord, and move on, ii) And pray that God would resolve those problems in the coming New Year.

The first scripture comes into my mind is Exodus Chapters 14- 15, which is the story that Israel people crossed the Rea Sea. It was the story of the miracle. As I looked back of this year, I saw that God had performed miracle in our lives. It did not need to be a big event like Moses opened the red sea, but it could be a small thing. The important matter was that God had done great things in our lives to save, rescue, protect, guide, and lead us with His unfailing love.

What he starts; he finishes (Philippians 1:6: "I am confident that he who began a good work in you will carry it on to completion until the day of Christ coming back or we reach to heaven.")

Protect
Guide
Love unfailingly

Because God chose you, He will forever keep you until you reach to His kingdom. Jesus is same yesterday, today and forever.

Now, the Israelites got the great victory at red river because God used the red river water amazingly. It was much more powerful than water-killer victory.

This teaches us that the barrier, block, and the curse to the Israelites- which is the outraged water of red river- became their protection and the strong weapon to wipe the enemies out.

Do you have obstacles that block your way? Do you experience the crisis now?

Those curses, blocks, crisis will turn as the opportunity and blessing to you. The pillar of the clouds, the pillar of fire, and the outraged water were all that God used to protect his people against enemies fiercely.

My prayer for you is that God blesses you and turn your crisis into the blessing as God had blessed the Israelites and changed the situation. God's wisdom and strength can make it possible for you.

God has many names: Shamma (God of Shepherd), Nisshi (God of victory), Jehova-Jareh (God of Provider), and Jehova-Sahlom (God of Peace). God's another name is God of Warrior.

When we are tired of fighting with our own strength and weary, God steps in and fights for us and gives victory for us.

The Lord is our boss, yet he fights for us because of His love and care for us. He wants to protect us from the enemies and give victory to us.

Always remember that our loving God fights for you and turn your crisis into a blessing, give protection for you.

The second story that comes in my mind as I prepare the sermon for the last day of the year was the story in 1st Samuel Chapter 7.

God, as the One who sovereigns our life, has intervened in our lives and has led us to the present situation in whatever areas of your life; marriage, career, family, location, and friendship. We have to trust that God is the one who leads our life to the present time and unto this situation.

Have you heard the word "Ebenezer"? You can find this word at 1st Samuel 7:10-12. It is the word composed by two meaning, which are 'Help' and 'Stone'. It was a remark that was inscribed on the stone. Samuel inscribed 'Ebenezer' when the Israelites had victory at the battle with the Philistines. And it means *"Thus far has the Lord helped us"*. Let me tell you this story briefly. Samuel had dual role both as judge and the prophet. He was a political and religious leader at the same time. While he was sacrificing the burnt offering, the Philistines sneaked in and came close to engage the Israel in the battle, but the Lord thundered in the loud thunder against the Philistines. The soldiers of Israel rushed out at Mizpeh and pursued the

Philistines along the way to a point below Bethcar and they had won the war there. *After this victory, Samuel took a stone and set it up between Mizpah and Bethcar and named it as "Ebenezer", which means, "thus far Yahweh has helped us." Samuel acknowledged that God led them to victory.* It was a very great event. It was not so difficult to admit that God's sovereignty was present at the time of victory. However, we have to admit God's sovereignty even at the time of lost because God is the one who guide us whether in our success or defeat.

Thus far the Lord has helped us:

Whether in time of sorrow, defeat/ or in time of success and victory, God our loving Father has lead, guide us and helped is to reach to now. Even in time that we were in crisis, God has helped us to turn those crises as the opportunity and blessing in 2018.Thus Far the Lord has helped us and He will lead, guide us with His Unfailing love

Our Lord, with his unfailing love will continue guide, lead, help us in the coming year of 2019.

CHAPTER 4
COMPASSIONATE LOVE OF GOD AND HIS FORGIVENESS GIVE HOPE

Truthful Love
John 3:16

JOHN 3:16 BEST EXPLAINS HOW MUCH God loved humankind. It says that God so much loved humankind that He gave His one and only begotten Son Jesus Christ to save humankind from sin, death, and fiery eternal judgment.

Therefore, first, true love is sacrificing. God expressed His true love toward us with the sacrifice of His Son.

One day a child asked her Sunday school teacher, "Teacher, how much does God love us?" The teacher opened his arms, stretched them wide, and said, "This much, and He died for you on the cross like this to show His love to you." That is what Jesus did to show you how much God loves you. Jesus came to this world as a king of kings. However, He was a savior king who suffered to redeem us and became a ransom for all of us.

There was a small aircraft crash once. The emergency team arrived to save the pilot and the passengers. However, when they arrived, they thought there could be no survivors with that hard of a crash. Everything smelled like burning already. Everything became ashes and smog. Yet they heard one baby crying in the midst of the smog. When the emergency medic team reached near the smog, they found one mother protectively embracing a baby. The mother died, and the baby survived. This baby was the only survivor when the aircraft clashed, because of the mother's sacrificial love.

It may be easy just to say, "I love you." However, true love should accompany sacrifice, commitment, and effort toward the beloved. True love brings pain.

Mother Teresa, who was awarded the Nobel Peace Prize in 1980 said, "True love hurts." She continued, "It hurt God when He gave His only begotten Son to the world; it hurt Jesus when He died on the cross; it hurt His Mother, Mary, to see her precious Son suffering on the cross."

Christ showed His sacrificial love on the cross. Christ suffered on the cross for us. Definitely, it was not because of His sin, it was for our redemption. But people responded differently. When Jesus hung on the cross, there were two criminals hung on each side. One of the criminals screamed and hurled insults at Christ, saying, "Aren't you the Christ? Then, save yourself and us."

Christ cried with a loud voice in His extreme suffering: *"Eloi, Eloi, lama sabachthani,"* which means, "My God, my God, why have you forsaken Me?" Hearing this, some people ridiculed Him: "Leave Him alone. Let's see if Elijah comes to save Him." However, some people who witnessed Christ's suffering and death on the cross realized Christ was their Messiah. One centurion and some other Roman guardians, seeing all the events that happened, exclaimed, "Surely, He was the Son of God!" And the criminal who hung with Christ on the other side rebuked the one who ridiculed Christ, "Don't you fear God? We are punished justly, for we are getting what our deeds deserve. But this man has done nothing wrong." He asked Jesus, "Jesus, remember me when you come into your kingdom." Jesus answered him, "I tell you the truth, today you will be with Me in paradise." On the cross in His extreme pain, Jesus gave hope to the one who was dying hopelessly and carried him to paradise. Jesus took all our sins, sorrows, and pains. He redeemed us. How could Jesus could show such genuine love and care for a hopeless person at the moment of His deep suffering and hurt? This shows Christ's sacrificial love for humankind.

Second, after sacrifice, true love is accepting others instead of rejecting them. One of humankind's deepest desires is the yearning for belonging. In Daniel Defoe's famous novel *Robinson Crusoe*, Crusoe experienced the hurt in human society and wanted to escape from people. He chose to live alone on an isolated island. However, he discovered one Friday that he should come back to society even though there still were conflicts in his relationships with others. Human beings need to belong to a group of people. Otherwise, they are too lonely to survive. At the same time, there is always hurt when people gather.

Live alone, or belong to society?

That is the question! That is the dilemma!

The answer would be to make an accepting society whose members could get along well and be happy together as they built up good relationships. The key is to love by accepting each other. That was the love that Jesus Christ showed. It was the love that God showed (Luke 15). Jesus accepted all: the lepers, the prostitutes, people who were born blind, uneducated people, fishermen, robbers, poor people, rich people, outcast people, and novel people as well.

How come people cannot accept each other? It could be because of their differences, pride, jealousy, and so on. The biggest reason could be zealousness. Rejection is the absence of compassion and the overflowing of zealousness. Joseph was the most beloved son among Jacob's sons. Jacob gave him the best clothes and showed his favor to Joseph. Jacob's showing favoritism was not wise. Yet the more serious problem was the zealousness with which Joseph's brothers turned on him. They rejected him as their blood, and their zealous response blinded them so that they could put their own blood in a dungeon, which should have killed him. With their zealous competitiveness, they caused their brother great misery. If they had just accepted Joseph as their brother and had been compassionate toward him, they would have loved him as the charming youngest.

Be merciful, be compassionate, and accept each other with the compassion of God. That is the love that Jesus showed us. Human beings are all like dust; no one could ever be perfect and blameless. So, all human beings are the object of His mercy, not competition. Psalm 103:13–14 says, "As a father has compassion on his children, so the Lord has compassion on those who fear him; for he knows how we are formed, he remembers that we are dust."

If we accepted each other with God's compassion, we would make a happy, holy city in this world like the one described in Isaiah 11:6–9: "The wolf will live with the lamb, the leopard will lie down with the goat, the calf and the lion and the yearling together; and a little child will lead them. The cow will feed with the bear, their young will lie together, and the lion will eat straw like the ox. The infant will play near the hole of the cobra, and the young child put his hand into the viper's nest. They will neither harm nor destroy on my entire holy mountain, for the earth will be full of the knowledge of the Lord."

Acceptance is best described in the novel *Les Miserables*. One priest's forgiveness and acceptance of Jean Valjean changed him into an honorable man. The priest's accepting this man as God's child changed his heart and Jean Valjean became a marvelous Christian. It was the same love that Jesus showed us. Jesus accepted the robber as His child and said, "You are with Me today in paradise." Christ will accept you as you are with His compassionate love.

I pray that God helps you realize how much He loves you by showing you His sacrifice and how He accepts you. I pray that God helps you to love each other with a sacrificial and accepting love.

For Reflection and Discussion

1. What do you do when you love someone? Think about those who sacrifice their lives for your wellness, health, and happiness. Discuss the first aspect of love, which is sacrifice.
2. Meditate on Jesus, who, in His time of suffering, gave the hope of eternal life to the man who was dying on the cross. Discuss the sacrificial love of Jesus Christ. Meditate on Psalm 103:13–14 and John 3:16, and think about Jesus Christ's sacrificial love for you.
3. Discuss the second aspect of love, which is acceptance. What are reasons why people cannot always accept each other? Think about Jesus, who accepts all people as children of God regardless of their backgrounds.

God's Unconditional Love Completes Our Lives
1 Corinthians 13:1–3, John 21, 1 John 4:7–12

John says, "Dear friends, let us love one another, for love comes from God. Everyone who loves has been born of God and knows God. Whoever does not love does not know God, because God is love. This is how God showed his love among us. He sent his one and only Son into the world that we might live through him . . . No one has ever seen God; but if we love one another, God lives in us and his love is made complete in us" (1 John 4:7–9, 12)

If you have someone whom you dearly love and she loves you as well, your life will be happy. There was a fisherman who always had to be at sea; he sometimes endured hard labors when he had to fight against the waves and winds. He sometimes felt miserable because of the hard life he faced, yet he said that he had a happy life because he had a loving wife who always waited for him. Counselor Gary Chapman said, "For love, we will climb mountains, cross seas, traverse desert sands, and even endure untold hardships. Without love, mountains become unclimbable, seas uncrossable, deserts unbearable, and hardships our plight in life."[20]

God loves us, and He wants us to love each other so we will have happy lives. Without love, especially the love of God, no one's life can be complete and be happy.

Paul said to his people, "If I speak in the tongues of men and of angels, but have not love, I am only a resounding gong or clanging cymbal. If I have the gift of prophecy and can fathom all mysteries and all knowledge, and if I have a faith that can move mountains, but do not have love, I am nothing. If I give all I possess to the poor and surrender my body to the flames, but have not love, I gain nothing . . . And now these three remain: faith,

---

[20] Gary Chapman, The Five Love Languages, (CHICAGO, IL: Northfield Publishing, 1992),

hope and love. But the greatest of these is love" (1 Corinthians 13:1–3, 13). Prophecy that can foresee what will happen in the future, giant faith that moves the mountain of tasks, and the ability to deliver persuasive speeches for thousands of people are admired gifts. Yet without love, all of those excellent things mean nothing, because love is the most valued gift in human life.

The word *love* is the most used word everywhere in human society because it is very important in our lives. However, its meaning is sometimes vague because everyone uses it with different meanings. In English, there is only one word, *love*, for all kinds of love. The Greek language uses more words for *love*, which diversifies its meaning so that it better matches its various settings.

First, *eros*: the love between loving mates. It is a romantic kind of love.

God has blessed humankind to have romantic love between mates from the beginning of creation, when He created Adam and Eve. Genesis says,

The Lord God said, "It is not good for the man to be alone. I will make a helper suitable for him" . . . But for Adam no suitable helper was found. So the Lord God caused the man to fall into a deep sleep; and while he was sleeping, he took one of the man's ribs and closed up the place with flesh. Then the Lord God made a woman from the rib he had taken out of the man, and he brought her to the man. The man said, "This is now bone of my bones and flesh of my flesh; she shall be called 'woman,' for she was taken out of man." That is why a man leaves his father and mother and is united to his wife, and they become one flesh. Adam and his wife were both naked, and they felt no shame. (Genesis 2:18, 19b–25)

As the man and woman fell in love, in eros, God blessed them to bring new children into this world. Two became one, a complete number.

God not only blessed human beings to have soul mates, but blessed us to multiply and have families. As families grow, they become tribes and continue to grow as nations.

Genesis 1:28 says, "God blessed them and said to them, 'Be fruitful and increase in number, fill the earth and subdue it. Rule over the fish of the sea and the birds of the air and over every living creature that moves on the ground.'"

This romantic love can grow into *philos, storge*, and *agape* love. If it stayed just as fleshly love, humankind would only be flesh.

The second kind of love is *philia*: friendly, mental love. Philia represents the love of truthful, meaningful friendship. The friendship between David and Jonathan is a good example of this kind of love. Jesus talked about this kind of love when He said: "Greater love hath no man than this that a man lay down his life for his friends." With friendship and deep bonds, people became mature and their lives become abundant.

The third kind of love is *storge*: the parent's love toward his children. Parental love makes it possible for children to grow up spiritually, mentally, and physically. This love is almost like God's *agape* love. It sometimes imitates God's unconditional love. There is a deep and abiding affection because the child is the parent's blood, his own life. That is how God created all of His creatures.

The fourth kind of love is *agape*: God's unconditional love. The most used word for love in the Bible is *agape*.

Jesus' disciples ran away to spare their lives when Jesus' life was in danger. After Jesus overpowered death and was resurrected, He visited His betraying disciples. At the beach of Galilee, they had a nice fish dinner together. After that, He had an intimate conversation about love with them, especially with Peter. Jesus asked Peter three times, "Do you love Me?"

> *When they have finished eating, Jesus said to Simon Peter, "Simon son of John, do you love me more than these?"*
>
> *"Yes, Lord," he said, "you know that I love you."*
>
> *Jesus said, "Feed my lambs."*
>
> *Again Jesus said, "Simon son of John, do you love me?" He answered, "Yes, Lord, you know that I love you." Jesus said, "Take care of my sheep."*
>
> *The third time he said to him, "Simon son of John, do you love me?"*
>
> *Peter was hurt because Jesus asked him the third time, "Do you love me?" He said, "Lord, you know all things; you know that I love you."*
>
> *Jesus said, "Feed my sheep." (John 21:15–17)*

In this conversation about love, Scripture uses two kinds of love. The first one is philos, and the second one is agape. The original Scripture uses *agape* in Jesus' first and second love question, but the third time He asks, He uses the word *philos*. However, Peter answered three times with *philos*.

Peter denied Christ three times even though he wanted to be loyal to Jesus. He thought that he could die for Jesus, yet he found out that he was a coward. He wanted to spare his life and ran away. He felt guilty and ashamed, and even more, he felt sorry that he lost his relationship with Jesus. He denied Jesus three times. Jesus then asked the love question three times. Why did Jesus ask three times whether Peter loved him? Jesus wanted Peter to restore the love relationship with Him. When Peter answered Jesus three times that he loved Him, he confirmed that he was still Jesus' loving disciple.

More importantly, he realized that God's unconditional love was given to him through Jesus Christ. He restored his faith that God granted him forgiveness. Agape love restored and completed him.

Just like Peter, we sometimes feel that we are not worthy to receive God's love: we feel worthlessness and guilt and have negative thoughts because of something we have done or not done. However, agape love, the unconditional love of God, covers all our sins, transgressions, and guilt. As the psalmist said in Psalm 103, you are forgiven.

Psalm 103:11–14 says, "For as high as the heavens are above the earth, so great is his love for those who fear him; as far as the east is from the west, so far has he removed our transgressions from us. As a father has compassion on his children, so the Lord has compassion on those who fear him; for he knows how we are formed, he remembers that we are dust."

The story of Jean Valjean in *Les Miserables* demonstrates what compassion means, what agape and unconditional love mean.

Let me summarize how these kinds of love affect our lives. We are born into this world by eros, nurtured by storge, matured by philia, and complete the wholeness of life by agape. No one has ever seen God, but God lives in us and His love is made complete in us if we love one another.

May the blessings of God be with you to have a wonderful mate, share philia love with friends, parent with storge love, and most of all, experience God's agape unconditional love that will complete your life!

For Reflection and Discussion

1. How can you have a happy life? What does love do for our happiness?
2. Read 1 Corinthians 13:1–3 and 13, and discuss the importance of love.
3. What is love? What are the four kinds of love that the Greek language has words for? How important are those four loves, and how do those loves nurture you?
4. Imagine that Jesus is asking you now, "Do you love Me?" and answer that question. Why did Jesus ask Peter that question three times?
5. Meditate on Psalm 103:11–13 and John 21. Why was God compassionate to humankind? What is unconditional love?

Forgive As the Father Forgives You
Luke 15:11–32, Matthew 18:21–35

Life is a continuous series of challenging problem solving projects. One of the biggest challenges is to forgive, because it is not easy to forgive those who hurt us. If people cannot forgive, there will be much sadness and devastation.

I have seen many people who have been hurt in their family relationships. What was the first incidence of murder? Cain and Abel, who were the first brothers of the human race, experienced the tragedy of murder. Family strife continued with Esau and Jacob and between Joseph's brothers. This kind of hardship continues even today. Do not be surprised when someone in your close family hurts you. Family conflict is common. However, if the rift occurs between the father, mother, and children, it affects everyone very seriously.

Here is part of a poem a youngster wrote and sent to Dr. James Dobson's Focus on the Family program:

"It was such a touchy topic.

Does a child understand the gradual separation of a woman and man? Flashbacks haunt my thoughts—those scary, scary words. Why can't I just erase the threats that I overheard? Mommy's body pushed; the vase that's on the floor; Mommy crying, in such pain. Dad runs out the door. I'm frozen in the recurrent scene—no crying or speaking. Why? I'm filled with fear and sorrow. But no tear slips from my eye"[21] (Dobson, 166).

The opposite of love is not hatred. The opposite of love is the attitude of "I do not care." That is why bad relationships and unforgiving spirits, especially in family relationships, brutalize our emotions so seriously.

What should we do to heal the brutalized emotions and hurt that was caused by our families' conflicts and fighting? The simple answer to that is forgiveness and reconciliation.

---

[21] Rolf Zettersten, Dr. Dobson: Turning Hearts Toward the Home, (Dallas, TX: W Publishing Group, 1992), p166.

Those two words are the best medicines to cure our hurt. One of the most important traits in a healthy family is the ability to forgive one another. It is very important to nurture forgiveness in family relationships. Forgiveness brings the family back together, and it cures the soul. That was the ministry of John the Baptist and Jesus Christ, and it should be the focus of our ministry as well. Malachi was the last prophet of the Old Testament who prophesied the coming of John the Baptist, the forerunner of our Lord Jesus Christ. He prophesied, "See, I will send the prophet Elijah to you before that great and dreadful day of the Lord comes. He will turn the hearts of the parents to their children, and the hearts of the children to their parents" (Malachi 4:5–6a). The heart of John the Baptist's ministry was about reconciling parents with their children. Christ, who came four hundred years following the silent period, was sent as our reconciler. Jesus came to this world to turn the hearts of mothers and fathers to their children and the hearts of the children to their parents. Jesus' ministry is to reconcile human beings with God the Father.

I will offer the secret of forgiveness in one simple sentence: "See God's big picture." When you learn to see God's big picture, you will start to successfully forgive others.

First, you should first see the big picture of God's providence in your life. God leads you the best way even though others intend to harm you or sometimes mistakenly misguide you. If you understand and believe His providential will, you will be able to see the big picture of God's unsearchable wisdom, and you will find out that God arranged all things to lead you the best way. If you are able to see that truth, you will be able to forgive those who hurt you.

In Genesis, there is a success story of forgiveness. As you know, Joseph experienced a hard life from when he was teenager until he became a prime minister. Joseph was once a slave, and at another time, a prisoner. He went through many difficulties and suffered anguish and emotional turmoil. Those hardships started because his brothers had been jealous of Joseph and sold him to the merchant of Arabia.

Eventually, Joseph became the prime minister of Egypt. Unexpectedly, his brothers had to stand before Joseph and bow to him. Recognizing that the powerful man who stood right in front of them, the prime minister of Egypt, was their mistreated brother, all of Joseph's brothers who had agreed to sell Joseph were afraid of his revenge. However, Joseph had already forgiven his brothers. In fact, Joseph could not control his emotions. He released all the pain and suffering that he had endured in the past and wept very loudly in front of them. As he wept, Joseph announced to his brothers, "I am Joseph! Is my father still living?" But his brothers were not able to answer him because they were still terrified at his presence. Joseph told them, "Come close to me . . . Do not be distressed and do not be angry with yourselves for selling me here, because it was to save lives that God sent me ahead of you." Joseph further explained that God had saved the world from hunger and preserved the tribe of Israel as a remnant on earth (Genesis 45:4–7).

Joseph again expressed his belief when he was reunited with his brothers: "You intended to harm me, but God intended it for good to accomplish what is now being done, the saving of many lives" (Genesis 50:20).

Can you see how Joseph could forgive his brothers? It was not just because of his generous heart and attachment to his blood. Joseph could forgive his brothers because he saw the big picture of God's providence. He understood how God amazingly arranged things in his life and brought the best out of it.

What do you see as your biggest tragedy and the person who causes you to experience the most hardship? Open your eyes; do you see how God leads you to the best possible situation?

If you capture the big picture of God, our mysterious and amazing guide, you can say that what almost could destroy your life causes you to become a successful person and leads you to the best situation. You will be able to forgive those who caused you trouble, just as Joseph was.

The second big picture that you should behold is the greatness of God's love, His big heart. To be able to forgive, your heart should be big as God's heart. Our heavenly Father expressed His compassion on us in Psalm 103:12–14, "As far as the east is from the west, so far has he removed our transgressions from us. As a father has compassion on his children, so the Lord has compassion on those who fear him; for he knows how we are formed, he remembers that we are dust." God compassionately forgives us because He has a big heart and understands that we are from the dust and therefore weak.

The story of the prodigal son is an awesome parable about a forgiving father. It illustrates the forgiving father and the return of the rebel. The prodigal son ran off to a far country and lived such a wild life. After he spent all his money, he came back to the father. He did not look like the same son any longer. He wore ragged clothes and looked miserable. But while he was still a long way off, his father recognized him and was filled with compassion for him. He ran to his son, threw his arms around him, and kissed him. The son said to him, "Father, I have sinned against heaven and against you. I am no longer worthy to be called your son." The prodigal son couldn't expect to get back his son-ship. He just wanted to live at his father's house and be fed. However, the father forgave the son and forgot all his sins. This father was like the father in Psalm 103:12–14.

The father said to his servants, "Quick! Bring the best robe and put it on him. Put a ring on his finger and sandals on his feet. Bring the fattened calf and kill it. Let us have a feast and celebrate. For this son of mine was dead and is alive again; he was lost and is found!" This father is our Father in heaven who forgives our sins and asks us to forgive each other.

Peter came to Jesus and asked, "Lord, how many times shall I forgive my brother when he sins against me? Up to seven times!" Jesus answered, "Not seven times, but seventy times seven." Then, Jesus told them a parable to explain what forgiveness is.

Therefore, the kingdom of God is like a king who wanted to settle accounts with his servants. As he began the settlement, a man who owed him ten thousand talents was brought to him. Since he was not able to pay, the master ordered that he and his wife and his children and all that he had be sold to repay the debt. The servant fell on his knees before him. "Be patient with me," he begged, "and I will pay back everything." The servant's master took pity on him, canceled the debt and let him go. But when that servant went out, he found one of his fellow servants who owed him a hundred denarii. He grabbed him and began to choke him. "Pay back what you owe me!" he demanded. His fellow servant fell to his knees and begged him. "Be patient with me, and I will pay you back." But he refused. Instead, he went off and had the man thrown into prison until he could pay the debt . . . Then the master [heard about this and] called the servant in. "You wicked servant," he said, "I canceled all that debt of yours because you begged me to. Shouldn't you have mercy on your fellow servant just as I had on you?" In anger his master turned him over to the jailers to be tortured, until he should pay back all he owed. (Matthew 18:23–34)

Jesus Christ, with His love and mercy, canceled all our debts— our great amount of debts. Yet, we sometimes hold a grudge against others about little things because we do not remember how great our debts are that God has cancelled. We become unmerciful to others.

Everyone makes mistakes. All have gone astray; all have sinned. Everyone hurts others; likewise, everyone is hurt by others: spouse to spouse, brother to brother, sister to sister, parents to children, children to parents, and so on. Therefore, understanding our frailty, our sinfulness, and looking at those who hurt or fail us with God's great compassionate heart will enable us to become generous and forgiving.

There was a young man who had just gotten a job and worked as an intern. He made many mistakes and wasted a lot of the company's money. After the internship was over, he thought he would be fired. However, the owner and board members of the company gave him another chance. Later on in his career, when he became a head administrator of a large medical center, he testified, "Because the board members and the chairman forgave me, allowed me to continue to work and gave me another chance, I became who I am now."

God doesn't only give us one more chance but chance after chance, always forgiving us and helping us start again. We all make mistakes. Because of our transgressions, we all crucified Christ. However, God continually gives us another chance with His forgiveness and unconditional love. Further along in Jesus' passion, when Pontius Pilate judged Him, the crowd kept on shouting, "Take Him away. Take Him away! Crucify Him." These were people that Jesus had served, healed, and fed. They had the choice of saving Jesus or crucifying Him. But they continued to cry out, "Crucify Him." They scorned and cursed Jesus. And yet, Jesus forgave them. Jesus, said, "Father, forgive them, for they do not know what they are doing."

Would you do the same thing to your blood before this year's over? If you haven't had the chance to forgive and reconcile with your kin, I encourage you to pick up the phone, call them, and have cheerful conversations with each of them, especially with your family members. Do not wait for them to call you; you do it first. Your forgiveness will give them joy; it will give you great relief from remorse, hurt, and sorrow. It will cure your heart and soul. Moreover, God the Father forgives you, so you should forgive. Our forgiveness changes us into new, loving, kind, and generous people.

For Reflection and Discussion

1. What is forgiveness? Why should we forgive each other? What would your forgiveness do for others and you? How can the brutalized emotions and hurt caused by conflicts be healed?
2. How can we forgive others? Discuss your experience trying to forgive someone who hurt you, whether you failed to forgive or succeeded. What makes you succeed at forgiving? If you failed, what makes it difficult for you to forgive someone who hurts you in your experience?
3. Discuss the author's two secrets for how you can forgive successfully.
4. Mediate on what Jesus said in His extremely painful moment on the cross: "Father, forgive them, for they do not know what they are doing."

The Joy of Finding the Lost
Luke 15, Matthew 18:11–13

There was a group of religious people who were segregated, especially outcast, and did not associate with any people who did not meet their standards. Their religious sect was the Pharisees. They were against Jesus because Jesus wanted to reach out to the outcast in His day. Luke 15 recounts three parables that Jesus shared in the context of the Pharisees' opposition and grumbling about Him associating with sinners (Luke 14:1, 5:30, 7:39).

Jesus gave three parallel parables about a lost coin, lost sheep, and lost son to teach that we should understand God's love for the lost and rejoice in finding the lost.

The real targeted audience of these parables was actually the Pharisees, who were described as those who worked hard and behaved decently and yet were reluctant to welcome the returned brother. Jesus' purpose of telling this parable was not to be judgmental but to help those people who never could grasp the meaning of grace to understand the heart of God, the Father, who is compassionate to the lost. Jesus also wanted them to have the privilege to experience real joy and join in the great work of God's redemption.

Three parables in Luke 15 speak of the same theme: God is seeking the lost and is joyful when he finds the lost. The first two parables are about a shepherd looking for the one lost sheep and a lady looking for a lost coin. The lost sheep and the lost coin signify the lost people, the sinners of those days. The third parable is about the father who is reunited with his prodigal son; two parables are about seeking and one is about waiting. I want you to see the connection between waiting and searching: waiting is strong expression of the love of the one who is seeking. The Lord was seeking and then waiting and again seeking for lost souls. God's unconditional love for lost people is well expressed in these parables, which amazingly illustrate God's love in three ways.

First, he was lost and now is found.

In the parable of the prodigal son, the father tried to persuade his first son that they had to accept the other son who came back after doing despicable things: "We had to celebrate and be glad, because this brother of yours was dead and is alive again; he was lost and is found" (Luke 15:31).

Human beings are lost. The Lord has been seeking and then waiting and again seeking the lost souls from the time when Adam and Eve were lost in the garden of Eden; "The Lord God called to the man, 'Where are you?'" (Genesis 3:9). From the time when Adam and Eve sinned and hid themselves from God, they were lost beings. From the time when the prodigal son left his father's house and lost his relationship with the father, he was lost. People are lost when they do not know the love of God and have lost their relationship with God.

Lost in Greek, is *apollumi*, which describes a thing that is not used or claimed; it refers to something no longer visible, known, possessed, or attainable. A lost person is one who is unable to find the way, confused, helpless, ruined, or destroyed physically, mentally, or morally. Lostness in the spiritual world goes little further than the literal meaning. It means anyone who is out of touch with the love of the eternal God. Lostness means separation, isolation, and alienation, being cut off from our true existence. One of the greatest evangelists in these recent centuries, D. L. Moody said, "I see every person as though he had a large L in the midst of his forehead. I consider him lost until I know he is saved."

Ernest Hemingway, who wrote "The Old man and the Sea," described an old man who caught a whale while fishing in his ragged, small fishing boat. He pulled the big whale as he fought against the waves of the outraged sea. The old man struggled to bring the whale to land. Although a shark attacked him on the way, he kept the whale successfully. Finally, he arrived on land and pulled out the whale. However, the only thing he could see was the whale's skeleton; the shark had eaten it all on the way.

Hemingway, although he was a famous and respected writer, shot himself in his head and killed himself. He was like Adam hiding behind the fig leaves, lost. People are lost if they are out of touch with the eternity and true love of God.

However, the good news is that God is desperately waiting for His children to come back and is looking for them like a tearful mother who lost her young boy.

God still remembers people who are lost and wants to find them. He feels a great sense of loss when His children are lost and do not come back to Him, as described in this parable of the lost son. The lost coin could be one of ten held together by a silver chain and worn on a headpiece to signify a woman was married. No one might have cared about the lost coin, as it did not have a lot of value, yet it was so valuable for this young married lady. Nobody cared about the prodigal son, because he was a despicable boy; maybe he got drunk all the time and associated with prostitutes. However, to his father, he was a dear son created in his own image. The image of the father's face, foot, and all spiritual, mental, and physical DNA were ingrained in this son— although some of it had faded because of the son's sinful life.

Second, there is joy in finding the lost.

Hole in one!

I could never forget the joy of the occasion when I played golf and hit a hole in one! It rolled somewhere, and I thought that it had gone off the green. I remember wondering, "Where is the ball? I cannot find it anywhere." I looked at everywhere! One of my friends said, "It is right here inside the hole. It rolled slowly and all of sudden disappeared. It was in the hole." Do you know how joyful it was to find the ball I thought I'd lost was in the hole?

The joy of the father was much more than that. Luke 15:20–22 reads:

> But while he was still a long way off, his father saw him and was filled with compassion for him; he ran to his son, threw his arms around him and kissed him. The son said to him, "Father, I have sinned against heaven and against you. I am no longer worthy to be called your son." But the father said to his servants, "Quick! Bring the best robe and put it on him. Put a ring on his finger and sandals on his feet. Bring the fattened calf and kill it. Let's have a feast and celebrate. For this son of mine was dead and is alive again; he was lost and found."

That was Jesus' joy when He was with sinners, tax collectors, prostitutes, outcast laborers, fishers, and zealots. He seemed not to be as pious as religious leader should be; rather, He spent time with a gaggle of outcasts. It reminded people of David, who joyfully danced without any skirts when he got God's lost ark back. Even his royal wife despised David at that time. The joyful father accepted and welcomed his formerly lost and prodigal son with a joyful heart; they shared tears and laughter together!

Jesus emphasized the clergyman's role in finding lost human beings in Matthew 18:10–13.

The New International Version (NIV) of Matthew 18:10–14 reads:

> See that you do not despise one of these little ones. For I tell you that their angels in heaven always see the face of my Father in heaven. [No verse 11.] What do you think? If a man owns a hundred sheep, and one of them wanders away, will he not leave the ninety-nine on the hills and go to look for the one that wandered off? And if he finds it, truly I tell you, he is happier about that one sheep than about the ninety-nine that did not wander off. In the same way your Father in heaven is not willing that any of these little ones should perish.

Many Bible versions of Matthew 18 leave out verse 11 as in this excerpt. But the King James Version includes verse 11, which reads; "For the Son of man is come to save that which was lost." Although Matthew 18:11 is not found in the earliest and best manuscripts, it may have been encouraged by the words of Luke 19:10 and added by a later scribe to provide a better bridge between Matthew 18:10 and the parable in Matthew 18:12–14. It is generally believed that the context of Luke 19:10 is Luke 18, which describes Jesus accepting Zacchaeus, whom had a high social status and whom everyone despised. However, it is safer to say that Matthew 18:11, which discusses the lostness of human beings, comes from the concept of Luke 15, which explains the father's unconditional love for his lost son.

The disciples, future spiritual leaders, learned from Jesus that they had to love the lost and people with low social statuses (Matthew 18:1–10). Matthew understood the human condition of lostness and God's heart toward the lost people to find them because of his personal experience and he described best it in Matthew 18:14: "Your heavenly Father do not want any of these little one to be lost." (author's paraphrase)

There was an occasion when the disciples asked the question, "Who is the greatest in the kingdom of heaven?" To answer, Jesus held a little child and said, "I tell you the truth, unless you change and become like little children, you will never enter the kingdom of heaven" (Matthew 18:1–3). Little children, people of low social status, and the poor were not welcome to society in Jesus' day—just like these days. Children sometimes were ignored and even not included in the count of family members. That was the context for Jesus' parable of the lost sheep.

Therefore, lost people could be people who are ignored and of low social status. Jesus said, "See that you do not despise one of these little ones. For I tell you that their angels in heaven always see the face of my Father in heaven" (Matthew 18:10).

Matthew included social embracement with spirituality. In verse 10, Matthew says that we should not ignore people of low social status. It is amazing to hear that even little ones have their designated angels who report to God the Father directly on how they are treated. Jesus reminds those who look down on people with low income or low social status that we all have our own angels to report to God in heaven on how we were treated.

Third, pardon, grace, welcome, and privilege.

The prodigal son did not expect to be pardoned. However, grace was given to him. Why? The father says, "For this son of mine was dead and is alive again; he was lost and is found. So, let us celebrate." The only condition for this forgiveness was that the father and son had a relationship. The father welcomed his son home and rejoiced just because his son was his own; it was his son, his life and blood.

The father's grace was expressed in three ways.

> - **Robe:** This was not just a regular robe; it was the best robe that was reserved for notable guests. The returned son was a notable guest.
> - **Ring:** By giving his son a ring, the father accepted him as his own, forgot what he had done, forgave all, and took him back.

> **Sandals:** Sandals were a luxury in those days; they were not for servants but for sons. Therefore, this gift signifies the father's full acceptance of his returned son.

The returned son did not deserve to get all of those nice gifts. The lost son was not significant enough to get this attention from his father. However, it was given by the grace of God. Just like the silver coin, the lost sheep, and the prodigal son, you may not be significant to others. But, you are significantly important to God, the Father. Therefore, God will be extremely joyful when He gets you back if you are lost. My prayer is that I could embrace the lost people in my ministry and look for them to return to God with the shepherd's heart and the father's broken heart. It is my prayer that today's ministers would have Jesus' shepherd heart for the lost people, outcasts, and sinners.

For Reflection and Discussion

1. Have you experienced the loss of something or someone valuable in your personal life? If you did, share your experience with the group.
2. Who are today's lost people?
3. Meditate on and discuss the father who was waiting for his lost son and joyfully welcomed him back home.
4. How do you treat the outcast or someone who has a lower social status than you?
5. What can you do to minister to lost people?
6. Meditate on Luke 15:20–24 and discuss what was unexpected about the father's welcoming of the prodigal son. What does this express about God's love for you?

CHAPTER 5

HOPE OF THE 21ST CENTURY: MESSIANIC MESSAGE OF THE NEW HOPE AND THE JUSTICE OF THE WORLD

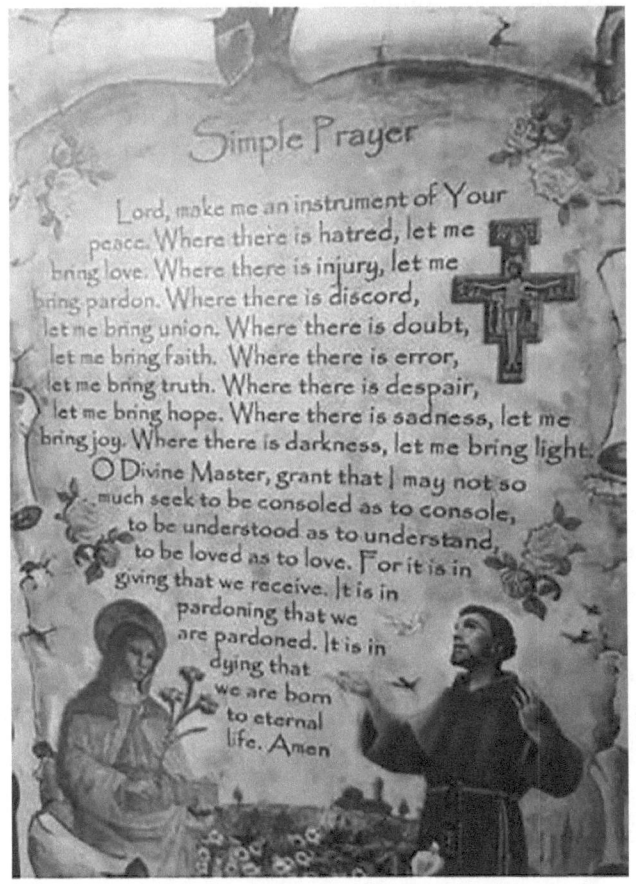

Pray for US Army to be used for God's work in keeping the Justice of the World

MOSES AND HIS SUCCESSOR, JOSHUA, HAD the same calling from God to call out his people from bondage to the Pharaoh and to lead them to the Promised Land, the land flowing with milk and honey. When God called each of them, they heard the voice of God saying, "Take off your sandals, for the place where you are standing is holy." The difference in calling Joshua, however, was that God first gave the mission to Joshua and called him later when he and his people approached the fortress of Jericho. The fortress of Jericho was the strongest city in the region, virtually impossible to conquer, yet it was the first gate through which God's people would gain access to his promises. If they could not pass through that gate, they would not even start to approach the land of promise.

Joshua met a man standing in front of him with a drawn sword in his hand, who turned out to be an angel. Joshua asked, "Are you for us or for our enemies?" Since God called him to lead his people and conquer the Promised Land, Joshua thought that the man with the sword came to be on his side and expected a positive answer from him. The angel's answer was totally unexpected.

"Neither," he said, "but as commander of the army of the Lord I have now come."

Hearing that, Joshua bowed down to the ground in reverence and asked the angel, "What message does my Lord have for his servant?"

The commander of the Lord's army replied, "Take off your sandals, for the place where you are standing is holy."

If this chaplain said today that the commander of the Lord's army is with the U.S. Army, many people would say the statement was not theological. Yet it is this chaplain's conviction and belief that God is the commander of the Lord's army and that he is with the U.S. Army. At the same time, one cannot ask if God is for or against one's side. The commander of the Lord's Army would give the same answer he gave to Joshua, "Neither."

Instead of Americans demanding for God to be with the U.S. Army, they should be with God, be loyal to him, and be willing to fight for him. With this kind of thinking, the chaplains of the U.S. Army will continue to be good moral advisers for the senior leaders of the Army and the nation.

World Evangelism and the Justice of the World Prayer for the World Evangelism and the Justice: BIBLICAL, THEOLOGICAL, THEORETICAL, AND HISTORICAL FOUNDATIONS[22]

The research foundations of this project include biblical, theological, theoretical, and historical areas, each of which will address spiritual leadership in the distinctive culture of the Army, pastoral care in the distinctive culture of the Army, moral advisement to leaders and soldiers, ministry in a multi-religious setting, and ministry in a multi- cultural/multi-racial setting.

Ministry in the U.S. Army setting is much different from ministry in local, denominational, or community churches. Military ministry has multi-spectrum aspects since the role of a U.S. Army chaplain is not just a preaching ministry, but ministry that includes planning, developing, and administering the Master Religious Program that provides counsel, pastoral care, and advice to commanders on religious, ethical, and moral issues as they

---

[22] Doctor of Ministry Project, Unites States Army Chaplains Ministry, Andrew Choi, Houston Graduate school of Theology, Houston, Texas May 2012. 10-17

affect the War Plan. Military ministry also is performed in a multi-racial and multi-religious setting.

Biblical Foundations

Old Testament Foundation

People misunderstand the Old Testament as the record of Hebrews who claimed God as only their God and, therefore, excluded other races. The Hebrew Scriptures, however, offer significant endorsement for extending open arms to many nations. The Pentateuch's endorsement for a multi-national ministry is shown, for example, when God first called Abraham: "The Lord had said to Abram, 'Leave your country, your people and your father's household and go to the land I will show you. I will make you into a great nation and I will bless you; I will make your name great, and you will be a blessing' " (Gen. 12:1-2).

Abram had a good life at Haran. His name at the time meant "honored father," yet he was still childless when he was seventy-four years old. What an irony that the man with the name "honored father" was actually childless. Whenever people called Abram by name, it would have reminded him that he was a childless, old man with no one to carry his name to the next generation. Abram lived at Harran when he was called, yet the Pentateuch (Josh. 24: 2-3; Gen. 14:3) emphasized that Abram's hometown was Ur, which was located east of the Euphrates River. Thus, Ur was the origin of the Hebrew nation, as the nation started with the tribe that crossed the river. When God called Abram, he had to leave his country, his hometown, and his kinfolk. That Abram followed God's calling to leave when he crossed the Euphrates River has significant meaning.

God called Abram out of Ur and sent him to the Promised Land so that he could single-heartedly follow God and become a blessing to all nations. It was through God's blessing of Abram's obedience that he became a source of blessing for many others. God further added to his blessing: "I will bless those who bless you, and whoever curses you I will curse; and all peoples on earth will be blessed through you." (Gen. 12:3).

The purpose of God's calling is to bless his people, yet it goes further; he blesses his people so they will become a source of blessing to others. Kenneth

Matthews emphasized that Abram is the dispenser of blessing for the nations and Abram has no exclusive claim on God's blessing. His calling is not to obtain a selfish blessing but rather to contribute to the blessing of others. God calls his people to become those who give joy and laugher to those who are depressed and sad, to give hope to those who despair, to strengthen those who are weak, and to give peace to those who have anxiety.

In the second part of the prophecy of Isaiah (chapters 40-66), one discovers the theme of comfort. God is the one who wants to bless all nations. The most significant scripture stating that God wants to bless multiple nations is found in Isa. 54:2-5:

Enlarge the place of thy tent, and let them stretch forth the curtains of thy habitations: spare not, lengthen thy cords, and strengthen thy stakes; For thou shalt break forth on the right hand and the left; and thy seed shall inherit the Gentiles, and make desolate cities to be inhabited. Fear not, for thou shalt not be ashamed: neither be thou confounded; for thou shalt forget the shame of thy youth, and shalt not remember the reproach of thy widowhood any more. For thy Maker is thine husband; the Lord of hosts is his name; and the Redeemer the Holy One of Israel; The God of the whole earth shall he be called (KJV).

A similar statement is found in Isa. 45:22: "Turn to me and be saved, all the ends of the earth: for I am God, and there is no other."

The following statement on Deutero-Isaiah, from James King West, holds that God's evangelical mission through Israel is universal and worldwide:

What the lifeless idols cannot offer their devotees, Yahweh provides. The incipient universalism of the Yahwist and Amos is here articulated in terms of a worldwide mission for Israel. Her whole history is a praeparatio evangelica for the salvation of the nations. The prophet thus manages to combine the finest sense of Yahweh's love for the elect people—the insights of Hosea and Jeremiah—with the clearest summons in the Old Testament to the whole race of men to come forward and accept their salvation.

Francis Dubose made a profound parallel statement with the interpretation of Isa. 66:19: "Other high points of the salvific sending are reached in the book of Isaiah. The Servant songs of Isaiah speak further of God sending the surviving remnant to be witness to many people, to declare his glory among the nations."

Additionally, in Walther Eichrodt's discussion of how the Israelite national hope could become the religious core of the whole salvation hope, he states:

This is to be found in the coming of Yahweh to set up his dominion over the world. This coming Yahweh was, however, already depicted at quite an early stage as the restoration of Paradise . . . God's actions burst all human scales of measurement.

If ministers follow the model and recommendation of the Old Testament, the biblical text shows examples and models of spiritual leadership and pastoral care in multi-racial settings; these are ministers who are called by God and please him by obeying their calling. The success of the ministry in the U.S. Army setting depends on having an unbiased and open mind toward all people, whether Hispanic, African- American, Asian, White, or any other racial ethnicity or culture.

New Testament Foundation

Jesus states in his supreme command: "Therefore go and make disciples of all nations, baptizing them in the name of the Father and the Son and the Holy Spirit" (Matt. 28:19).

John MacArthur states that how Christians understand all the passages of Matthew's gospel depends on their understanding of Matt. 28:16-20, which is Jesus' supreme command to reach out to all the people of the nations.

Apostle Paul, who states, "The scripture foresaw that God would justify the Gentiles by faith, and

announced the gospel in advance to Abraham: 'All nations will be blessed through you'" (Gal. 3:8) and "To the weak I became weak. I have become all things so that by all possible means I might save some" (1 Cor. 9:22). MacArthur's commentary on 1 Cor. includes not only his exegesis of the scripture but also an in-depth study of the church of Corinth. There, he explains why Christians should be concerned for people who have weak faith. He also explains that Paul identified with those who had weak faith, and he became all things to all men that he might save some. Paul, who held the strong theological view that Jesus was the only way for the salvation of the world, lowered himself and became a weak person to identify with weak persons who could not yet understand and accept Christ. He became a Jew for the Jew; he became a Greek to the Greeks. Through his humility, he wanted ultimately to win their souls. He did not put any unnecessary barriers or practices before the un-churched foreigners, so they could more easily approach Christ with an open mind, without feelings of exclusion.

Martin Luther King, Jr. observed with strong words that people were the most segregated when gathering for church services on Sunday morning:

We must face the fact that in America, the church is still the most segregated major institution in America. At 11:00 on Sunday morning when we stand and sing and Christ has no east or west, we stand at the most segregated hour in this nation. This is tragic. Nobody of honesty can overlook this. Now, I'm sure that if the church had taken a stronger stand all along, we wouldn't have many of the problems that we have. The first way that the church can repent, the first way that it can move out into the arena of social reform is to remove the yoke of segregation from its own body. Now, I'm not saying that society must sit down and wait on a spiritual and moribund church as we've so often seen. I think it should have started in the church, but since it didn't start in the church, our society needed to move on. The church, itself, will stand under the judgment of God. Now that the mistake of the past has been made, I think that the opportunity of the future is to really go out and to transform American society, and where else is there a better place than in the institution that should serve as the moral guardian of the community; the institution that should preach brotherhood and make it a reality within its own body.

If evangelists continue to use culturally exclusive practices, then people will turn away and Christianity will not be free to communicate its truth and the gospel to the people. To become more effective and inclusive as Jesus did when he came to earth in human form, including Samaritans in his ministry (e.g., John 4:5-24), Christian ministers should become equally available to all races.

Jesus said, "God so loved the world" (John 3:16).

Commenting on John 3:16, which is the focal verse of the gospel, Bruce Barton and co-authors David Veerman and Neil Wilson, in a commentary on the book of John, explain why Christians should reach out to all people: "God's love is not static or self-centered; it reaches out and draws others." God's love is not just for Christians but also for the world, which means that his love reaches out to every kind of person in the world. In the same way, it is imperative that Christians should reach out to all people.

God's love for humankind was universal, but it was costly. In his exegesis of John 3:16, Gerald Borchert explains the theological perspective of self-giving and sacrificial love to people. The cost to God was the life of his only begotten Son, which sacrifice was not only for one particular group of people or sect, not only for one race, but rather it was for all people in the world—Hispanic, African-American, Asian, Caucasian, and all others.

When Christian ministers show the love of God to all people without prejudice, that action alone will help lead them to become followers of Christ. That is why Paul warned to have a good and harmonious relationship with all people whenever possible. Rom. 12:18 reads, "If it is possible, as far as it depends on you, live at peace with everyone." MacArthur states that "everyone" includes even the meanest and the most undeserving, "Everyone" also indicates accepting and loving those people who have a completely opposite belief system and way of life. In a perfect and ideal world, Christians should have no conflict with such people. The world is much less than perfect, however, and Jesus still wants his people to be at peace with everyone whenever possible. That is the ultimate calling for the minister of the Christ, and it will require an inclusive attitude, and generosity and respect for all people.

It is common knowledge that some Christians have an exclusive perspective toward others, focusing on their own interests instead of the interests of others. Some have gone so far as to extend this kind of self-centered thinking into evangelism in such a way that it ends up looking more like imperialism than evangelism, which means to conquer others' minds and spirits in order to dominate them. The biblical intent of evangelism, however, seems to be much different from such a conquering view. God's intent is first to love and care for and then seek and find the lost. Only following God's intent to care for and seek the lost will bring about successful biblical evangelism.

Even so, Army chaplains need to know that they are the moral advisors to their commanders and decision makers at all levels. They will be called upon to ensure that an Army operation is a just cause.

Augustine of Hippo (A.D. 354-430) was concerned with the evilness of the human mind rather than the evilness of war. In a letter to Faustus, he wrote that when soldiers and leaders were involved in a war, they should not forget their moral responsibility:

What is the evil in war? Is it the death of some who will soon die in any case, that others may live in peaceful subjection? The real evils in war are: love of violence, revengeful cruelty, fierce and implacable enmity, lust for power. Good men undertake such wars, when they find themselves in such position as regards the conduct of human affairs that might conduct them to act, or to make others act, in this way.

Former Chief of Chaplains of the U.S. Navy, Louis Isaisello, wrote in his dissertation on just war about the responsibility of religious leaders as moral advisors: "This author hopes to provide some guidance to warriors, and especially their senior leaderships, concerning the relevance of just war theory."

When the ship is going to the wrong way, everybody in the ship is going the wrong way. If the ship sinks, all people in the ship will sink. Likewise, when the country does not go the right way, the religious leaders will sink with the country even though they are doing righteous ministry for their people. Therefore, it is the student's belief that Army chaplains should pray for the high decision makers to have sound judgment as they weigh the factors of a just cause. They also should be ready, as moral advisors and pastors, to provide wise counsel for the senior leaders and warriors.

Relevant Personal History of the Author

Korean War boy became the US Army Chaplain and worked as the NATO (North Atlantic Treaty Organization) Community Chaplain

The purpose of writing his personal story was to connect the author's convictions and life experience to explain why he believes in the Army chaplain's role. His life experience formed and developed his ministry philosophy.

He was born on December 16, 1952, during the Korean conflict. He actually was born in Pusan and, when he was three months old, his family moved from Pusan (far southern part of Korea) to Seoul (Capital city, north side of South Korea). At this time, the U.N. had a victory over the communist invaders. Seoul became his hometown.

He remembers the story of his aunt whom he never saw. It was around the time when the barrier (38th latitude) between North and South was going to be established. The peace treaty between the U.N. and the Red forces of communism made two separate nations from one race. His aunt and uncle were prospective young politicians. The North Korean government kidnapped them just before the 38th barrier was drawn between North and South Korea. People could not travel between the North and South because of the Iron Curtain. This author heard that his grandmother missed her daughter so much that she risked crossing the bridge between North and South Korea. She tried to find her daughter this way many times. So many US Army young Soldiers and UN forces from 16 countries of the world sacrificed shed their precious blood to save the Republic of Korea at 6.25 1950 Korean war.

Author inserting here the story of the US Army Chaplain Kapaun who awarded Medal of Honor for his sacrificial service at the Korean War.

Medal of Honor Awarded to Korean War Chaplain
By Jackie Calmes
April 11, 2013

WASHINGTON — Supporters of the Rev. Emil J. Kapaun, an Army chaplain who died a prisoner in the Korean War, are still working to have him declared a Catholic saint for his lifesaving ministrations to them. But for now, they have the satisfaction of seeing him posthumously awarded the Medal of Honor at the White House.

In an East Room ceremony on Thursday, President Obama presented the blue sash and five-pointed star to an emotional Ray Kapaun, a nephew. At 56, the nephew has been alive for less time than his uncle's comrades have labored to get recognition for their chaplain, who died nearly 62 years ago, at the age of 35, in a prisoner-of-war camp.

"This is an amazing story," Mr. Obama said. "Father Kapaun has been called a shepherd in combat boots. His fellow soldiers who felt his grace and his mercy called him a saint, a blessing from God. Today, we bestow another title on him—recipient of our nation's highest military decoration."

In this copy of a photograph on display at Kapaun Mt. Carmel Carmel Catholic High School in Wichita, Kap., a wounded soldier is helped by Army Chaplain Emil Kapaun during the Korean War.[23]

---

[23] https:///www.npr.org/search 'He Saved Hundreds': Army Chaplain Gets Medal Of Honor April 11, 2013. (Accessed on 11/21/2019)

Hope From the Garden of Eden to The End of the Patmos Island

Korea with the US Army: Go Together(함께 갑시다)[24]

36,574 precious sons of the United States' citizen sacrificed their life to keep the freedom and the democracy of ROK. 628,833 United Nations from 16 countries shed their precious blood to save Korea from the China, Russia, and North Korea communist' brutal invasion at Korean War 1950-1953.

He firmly believes that United States and Republic of Korea alliance is the God's providence to protect the democracy, Christianity in the Republic of Korea and US continue to be the leader of keeping Justice, Freedom, Democracy, Christianity of the world.

Author's grandmother also told the story of his grandfather, who died during the war of independence from Japan. His grandfather died when he was only twenty-nine years old, and his grandmother remained a single mother after that. She was always proud of her husband and frequently told

---

[24] 2nd Infantry Division stationed at South Korea motto. Go Together: 함께 갑시다

the story of the author's grandfather to him. His grandfather was a hero to the author because of his patriotism. His uncle and his father had much trouble and pain when the Japanese occupied the Korean peninsula. The Japanese forced all Koreans to change their names to Japanese names in order to destroy their identities. His uncle and his father never changed their names because their names came from their father and family names were sacred to them. They suffered many years in jail for keeping their names.

Until he turned forty, this author did not realize how much his father's and grandfather's generations suffered because of communism and the imperialism of the Japanese. He has great respect for his father and mother's generation and how they raised him to be a good citizen in spite of the difficult circumstances of rearing children during war. The author's parents taught him the value of family, country, honest work, and education. He remembers his father teaching him never to hate humans, even those who hurt him.

Childhood Formative Events Affecting Pastoral Functioning

His painful childhood experiences and the influence of his father form the core of this chaplain's religious heritage and theological understanding of the ministry. The following elements helped him to become a chaplain in the military setting.

Sorrow and Pain.

He experienced sorrow and the pain of poverty in his childhood, which helped him to become a sympathetic person. He is approachable and an active listener; therefore, people feel comfortable to open up and talk with him about their problems.

Religious Heritage.

His father always clung tightly to his faith, which brought hope even in times of depression. His actions and his optimistic view transferred to his son and formed the hope that gives him his reason to live. Optimism and hope are reflected in this chaplain's ministry style. When soldiers come for counseling during their crises, he always encourages them to have hope.

Calling to the Ministry of Gospel

The author's early ministry started when he was a senior in high school. He started his involvement in the Sunday school ministry as soon as he joined the church—even though he did not know Christ yet.

In his freshman year of college, he became involved in student demonstrations against his government's policies regarding Japan. He was severely injured by chemical tear gas powder that mixed with the rain and washed over his body while he was protesting.

While he was in the hospital, he experienced conversion and accepted Christ as his Lord and Savior. The Holy Spirit convicted him of his sin and made him aware of Christ's suffering. The Spirit made him realize that Christ's pain and death on the cross was to redeem him from sin. The experience of severe physical pain helped him understand the depth of God's redemptive love. He also realized that societal reform can be achieved only when each individual is reformed. Since his conversion experience, he has become a devoted Christian. While attending Seoul National University, he was deeply involved in the student evangelism movement.

The author was called to the ministry when he was a senior at college. Jesus' supreme command of world evangelism convicted him to devote his life to world missions. (Matthew 28:16-20) After graduation, instead of pursuing a career, he devoted his life to student evangelism as a "tentmaker" staff minister.

He came to the United States in 1983 because he wanted to reach to all races—not just the Korean people—with the word of God. When he first came to the U.S., he experienced many difficulties because of his language barrier, cultural differences, and financial hardships.

Calling to the United States Army Chaplain Ministry

He entered Golden Gate Baptist Theological Seminary in 1988 and graduated in 1992 with a Master of Divinity degree. While attending seminary, a recruiting chaplain came to his school and introduced him to military ministry. This student accepted being a military chaplain as his calling, because he thought that the military would be a perfect setting for ministry to all races, which had been his goal and dream.

He joined the Army as an active duty chaplain on July 17, 1994, and began service as a chaplain for the 204th Forward Support Battalion in Fort Hood, Texas. He stayed out in the field with soldiers on many occasions, which provided opportunities for him to meet with many young soldiers. It was a rewarding ministry. He was the agent of God's word, hope, and comfort when the soldiers had difficulties in their lives. One day, a strong sergeant, who never showed his emotions, came to his HAMMVE (Army Field Truck) at midnight. He had just lost his dear brother, and he was shaken and filled with grief. He asked this chaplain, "Am I shaking? Is it okay for a soldier to cry?" Giving comfort and encouragement during such a time of deep depression is this chaplain's gift and mission.

Unique Experiences in Ministry

The following events were unique in this chaplain's ministry in the Army while he was assigned to NATO (North Atlantic Treaty Organization) headquarters (HQ) in Brussels, Belgium.

One of the events that this student experienced in his role as an ethical advisor was when a young captain presented an article about "Just War" to the commander of the NATO HQ. It was the day before the U.S. air strike on Yugoslavia. The day this author visited the senior leader who had the most influence regarding this decision happened to be the day before the action. This author's visit to NATO HQ Commander LTG at Brussels, Belgium was purely to perform his chaplain role as moral adviser.

CHAPTER 6
THE POWER OF GOD THAT STRENGTHENS YOU

MOSES LEADING THE ISRAELITES CROSSING THE RED SEA[25]

---

[25] https://www.google.com/search?q=moses+divided+red+sea& (accessed on December 31, 2016)

God's Power Makes It Possible for the People of Israel to Cross the Red Sea
Exodus 14, 15:1–18, Psalm 136:12-15

THE PEOPLE ISRAEL CROSSING THE RED Sea story tells us that crisis and difficulties can be changed as the opportunity and blessing.

We all faces crisis, whether big or small, whether as the level of nation, or family, or individual meets Crisis sometime in our life. There are many kinds of crisis: economic crisis, spiritual crisis, political crisis, mid-life crisis, identity crisis, etc.

Some people collapse when they faces crisis, some people grow up, become strong, even and get the new opportunity, reach to the new horizon of their life as they overcome the crisis (adversity, trial, difficult life situation). It is like the eagle flying higher when they faces the strong storm against them, spread their wings wider to the coming winds and let it fly them very high. Flying eagle uses the wind as their opportunity to fly higher. During the Cuban crisis, former president, John F. Kennedy when he faced the challenge of Cuban crisis says the word-危機(Crisis, Opportunity) We GI (危機), which means that the Crisis as the Opportunity.

The Cuban Missile Crisis[26]

For thirteen days in October 1962 the world waited—seemingly on the brink of nuclear war—and hoped for a peaceful resolution to the Cuban Missile Crisis.

In October 1962, an American U-2 spy plane secretly photographed nuclear missile sites being built by the Soviet Union on the island of Cuba. President Kennedy did not want the Soviet Union and Cuba to know that

---

[26] https//www.jfk.library.org/JFK0in-History/Cuban-Missile-Crisis (accessed on Jan 3, 2017

he had discovered the missiles. He met in secret with his advisors for several days to discuss the problem.

After many long and difficult meetings, Kennedy decided to place a naval blockade, or a ring of ships, around Cuba. The aim of this "quarantine," as he called it, was to prevent the Soviets from bringing in more military supplies. He demanded the removal of the missiles already there and the destruction of the sites. On October 22, President Kennedy spoke to the nation about the crisis in a televised address.

Today's story, the Israelites crossing the Red sea tells us that the Crisis could be the way of opening the opportunity.

When the tribe of Israelites arrived in Egypt as immigrants, their numbers were only seventy. Since Joseph was the second most powerful man of the nation, the tribe of Jacob, which became the nation of Israel later on, could occupy the best land for cultivation and agriculture. This region was named Goshen and was located on the lower part of the Nile river. While their brother Joseph and his king ruled Egypt, they had blessed and good lives. Jacob's tribe lived there for generations, approximately 430 years. The first generation had good lives, and God blessed them to multiply to have many descendants. When the Israelites started to outnumber the native Egyptians and exceedingly multiplied to fill the land of Egypt, the new king who did not know Joseph worried that the prospering Israelites would conquer and take over their land. From that time, the new king persecuted them and made all the Israelites, old and young, men and women, slaves. In these modern days, people are amazed at the grand construction of the Pyramids in Egypt. They were built with the tears and sweat of Israelite slave laborers.

The Israelites groaned because of hard labor and persecution. Their tears and groans reached God. God heard them and sent them a liberator, Moses. He led the Israelites' exodus so that they could get freedom and could march to the Promised Land. Counting only the young men, the number of the Israelites would have been around 600,000. So, the total population could have been 2 million. They also had large numbers of cattle. The large number of people, including the cattle, left Egypt and marched through the Sinai wilderness toward Canaan, the Promised Land. As they left slavery, they were so excited by the dream of new lives in the new land. They already started to breathe the freedom. Think about this fantastic scene. The people who first experienced this freedom were overjoyed. They could have thought that that was it. They never expected or predicted the coming trial.

However, the trial visited them. In front of them lay the Red Sea, and the sea raged. They were blocked and could not find the way to continue on to the Promised Land. Leaving Egypt was only the start of their freedom; they had to cross the river to continue on.

There is always a river that we have to cross in our lives. That is life. What kind of river do you have to cross today?

What expectation do you have for the coming days?

To make things worse, the Pharaoh, with six hundred of his best-trained chariots, pursued the Israelites. They were trapped between the Sea and the onrush of Egyptians. As the Egyptian army approached them, the Israelites trembled and feared. Their enthusiasm and hope for the new life all of a sudden changed to fear and regret. They were so terrified that they even said to Moses, "We are dead meat; did you take us out to this wilderness because there were no graves in Egypt?" This is the situation: they could not go forward or return back. If they choose to go forward, the outraged sea would have swallowed them. If they chose to go backward, the Egyptian troops would have killed all of them. They had only one other option, if they were able; that is to go up to the sky. Yet, they could not.

No solution.

No way.

You are trapped.

We sometimes are in a situation in which we cannot move forward or withdraw backward. What can we do then?

Shall we see what happened, then, to the Israelites?

Moses told the terrified people "Do not be afraid. Stand firm, and you will see the deliverance the Lord will bring you today. The Egyptians you see today you will never see again. The Lord will fight for you; you need only to be still."

Psalm 46:20 says, "Be still, and know that I am God." You need only to be still!

That is all we can do. That is all we need to do.

The peace that God gives you is all you need in times of trouble. You can have peace in your mind because God will fight for you, and His power and knowledge transcend all things. His knowledge and wisdom are above and beyond our understanding. He resolves our problems with methods we could never figure out. Paul, who was in prison and did not know what would come next to his life, said, "Do not be anxious about anything, but in everything, by prayer and petition, with thanksgiving, present your requests to God. And the peace of God, which transcends all understanding, will guard your hearts and your minds in Christ Jesus" (Philippians 4:6–7).

The subject word here in verse 7 is the peace of God because the peace in our heart is so important.

When your heart fills with anxiety and fear, and stresses wake you up even in at midnight, shake your hard head; you may still not be able to figure the situation out.

Yet when God's Spirit reins in your heart, you will experience His reserved peace. Jesus slept in the midst of a storm because He had the peace of God in his heart. We also could have good sleep and serenity in the midst of a strong storm. We need good sleep in these days of economic slump. In times of trial, all we need to do is trust God, be still, and have peace in our hearts.

Sing a song, "When Peace like a river . . ."

At Moses' signal, God sent a strong wind all night, and it drew back the waters. The Red Sea opened, and the Israelites crossed as if they were walking on the land. The pursuing Egyptians, however, were not so fortunate; their chariot wheels mired in the soft ground of the Red Sea. That day, Yahweh rescued Israel from the Egyptians, and Israel saw the Egyptians lying dead on the shore.

Listen to the phrases that Moses and the Israelites sang at that time:
"The Lord is my strength and my song; He has become my salvation . . . Your right hand, O Lord, was majestic in power. Your right hand, O Lord, shattered the enemy . . . The enemy boasted, 'I will pursue, I will overtake them' . . . But you blew with your breath, and the sea covered them. They sank like lead in the mighty waters . . . You stretched out your right hand and the earth swallowed them. *In your unfailing love you will lead the people you have redeemed. In your strength you will guide them to your holy dwelling"* (Exodus 15:2, 6–7, 9–10, 12-13, emphasis added).

Throughout their history, the Israelites looked back to this great deliverance as the consummate event by which they became the people of God. It also was the primary example of God's redemptive purposes for them.[27] More importantly, this story foreshadowed the story of Jesus Christ, who delivered of human beings from the power of death and sin.

Through this miracle, what do we know of who God is?

First of all, God is the God of redemption, and His love is forever (Exodus 15:13).

The Israelites not only rejoiced in their deliverance from the enemy and their crossing of the Red Sea, but they also were glad that they discovered their identity as a beloved and redeemed people of God. They were so glad that they were not slaves. God and the Israelites have a special relationship, the Father to His children; they have had a covenant relationship of "I and Thou" not as "I and it", that Martin Buber defined the relationship[28], since the Israelites were redeemed. Redemption gives them the right to reclaim their position as free men and women and restore their relationship with God.

---

[27] William Sanford La Sor, David Allan Hubbard, and Frederic William Bush, Old Testament Survey, The Message, Form, and Background of the Old Testament, (Grand Rapids, Michigan: William B. Eerdmans Publishing Company1982), 143.

[28] Martin Buber (Hebrew: מרטין בובר; February 8, 1878 – June 13, 1965) was an Austrian-born Jewish philosopher best known for his philosophy of dialogue, . . . en.wikipedia.org/wiki/Martin_Buber (accessed on August 28, 2011).

Hope From the Garden of Eden to The End of the Patmos Island

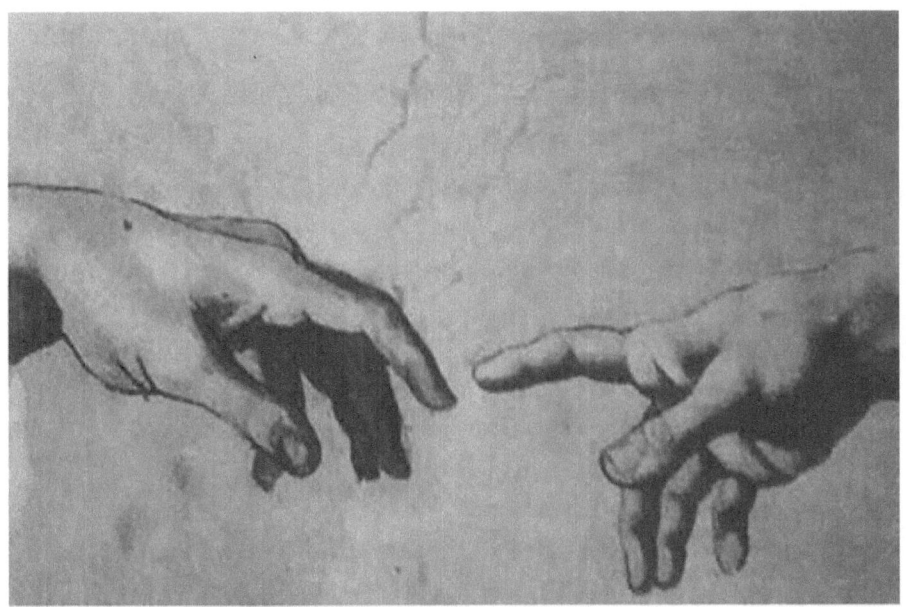

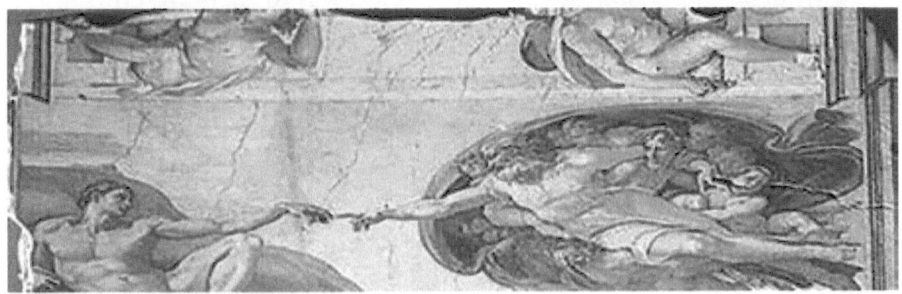

When the Israelites lived as slaves, they lost their identity, dignity, and self-image as God's people. When God freed them and passed over them with the price of the blood of the lamb, they again became a covenant people who had God's promise: the dignified image of God was in their hearts.

Exodus chapter 11and 12 described this Passover history. The king of Egypt, Pharaoh, did not want to let the Israel people to do exodus. He did not let the Israelites to become free people, and serve the Lord, Yahweh. To force Pharaoh to release the Israelites, God allowed the 10 disasters fell upon Egypt. The last punishment was the death of every first-born sons and first-born males of animals. Moses, in Exodus 11:4- 5, warned to Pharaoh: 'God will send the angels of death to all over the country of Egypt in the midnight and kill every first born-sons, from the prince to the first-born of servants, even to the first-born of beasts." (author's paraphrase) However, God wanted to save his children from the death angels and gave them instruction to get the blood of the lamb to put it in the door frame. It was to pass over the judgment of death. As God sent the angels of death overshadowed the whole country of Egypt in the midnight, the death angel passed over when they saw the blood of the lamb in the door frame of Israelites. The power of death just passed over, gave the children of God pardon from the power of death and gave them free. (Exodus 12:13) That was Passover. Likewise, Jesus Christ came to the human kind as the Lamb of God for the Passover. God restored the image of God in our hearts when He put all our infirmities and sins on Jesus, the Lamb of God; He redeemed our position as His own children.

This experience of deliverance, of crossing the Red Sea, gave them confidence that God would love them eternally and that His unchanging, unfailing, forever love would follow them.

This delivered people described who God was to them in terms of His "unfailing love." This means that God's love is forever, unchangeable, and trustworthy.

Here is a good definition of good person: a person whose love is trustworthy, unfailing, and stable. God is a good God.

What He starts; He finishes (Philippians 1:6).

God is good because He is unchangeable, unfailing, steady, and forever. Once He saves you, He will keep on loving you (2 Timothy 1:12).

The great deliverance story of the Passover and God's children crossing the red-sea convinces us that our God is who:

Protect.

Guide.

Love unfailingly.

Because God chose you, He will forever keep you until you reach His kingdom. Jesus is the same yesterday, today, and forever.

Second, God is the Almighty who turns a crisis and curse into an opportunity and blessing for His people.

It is amazing to see how God does that.

Hope From the Garden of Eden to The End of the Patmos Island

The outraged waves of the Red Sea were certainly the barrier, blocking their way. They could had said, "I wish I did not face this problem, the water blocking our way."

Let's see what happened. Moses opened Red sea.

Exodus 14:27–29 says, "Moses stretched out his hand over the sea, and at daybreak the sea went back to its place. The Egyptians were fleeing toward it, and the Lord swept them into the sea. The water flowed back and covered the chariots and horsemen—the entire army of Pharaoh that had followed the Israelites into the sea. Not one of them survived. But the Israelites went through the sea on dry ground with a wall of water on their right and on their left."

Now, the Israelites had the great victory at the Red Sea because God used the water amazingly. It was much more powerful than the Battle of Salsu.

This teaches us that the barrier, block, and curse to the Israelites became their protection and the strong weapon to wipe the enemies out.

Do you have obstacles that block your way? Are you experiencing a crisis now?

Those curses, blocks, and crises will turn into opportunities and blessings to you. The pillar of clouds, the pillar of fire, and the outraged water were all that God used to protect His people against enemies— and He used them fiercely.

My prayer for you is that God blesses you and turns your crisis into a blessing. God's wisdom and strength can achieve this.

Third, God is a mighty warrior who fights for you.

As the people looked at the Red Sea event, they saw God as the mighty warrior who fought for them; "the Lord is a warrior; the Lord is his name. Pharaoh's chariots and his army he has hurled into the sea. The best of Pharaoh's officers are drowned in the Red Sea" (Exodus 15:3–4).

"In the greatness of your majesty you threw down those who opposed you. You unleashed your burning anger; it consumed them like stubble" (Exodus 15:7).

God has many names: Shamma (shepherd God), Nisshi (God of victory), Jehova-Jareh (provider God), and Jehova-Shalom (God of peace). Another of God's names means warrior God.

When we are tired of fighting with our own strength, God steps in, fights for us, and is victorious.

The Lord is our boss, yet He fights for us because of His love and care for us. He wants to protect us from our enemies and give us victory.

In these days of economic crisis, when people lose their houses and jobs, remember that our loving God fights for you and turns your crisis into a protective blessing for you.

That was Paul's confidence when he was out of strength, as expressed in his letter to the Romans: "If God is for us," his letter asks, "who can be against us?"

And we know that in all things God works for the good of those who love him, who has been called according to his purpose. (Romans 8:28)

What, then, shall we say in response to this? If God is for us, who can be against us? He who did not spare his own Son, but gave him up for us all—how will he not also, along with him, graciously give us all things? (Romans 8:31–32)

No, in all these things we are more than conquerors through him who loved us. For I am convinced that neither death nor life, neither angels nor demons, neither the present nor the future, nor any powers, neither height nor depth, nor anything else in all creation, will be able to separate us from the love of God that is in Christ Jesus our Lord. (Romans 8:37–39)

For Reflection and Discussion

1. What was the blessing Jacob's tribe received when they immigrated to Egypt by Joseph's invitation? What problem did they face after Joseph's death? To save them, what did God arrange for them?
2. On the way to exodus, what problems did they encounter? What barriers blocked their way?
3. What would you do if you were, like the Israelites, trapped between the Red Sea and the chasing Egyptian "Special Chariot Forces"?
4. What kind of barriers blocks your way?
5. Why was their deliverance from their enemies and their crossing the Red Sea, which should have been impossible, such a memorable event to the people Israel?
6. What can you learn about God through how He delivered them from adversity? How did God turn the crisis into an opportunity at the Red Sea? Expect and experience that crisis you face today turning into an opportunity in your future.
7. Meditate on Romans 8:31–39 and how God opened the Red Sea. Trust God, who would fight for you too, and experience the victory in your life.

God's Almighty Power Makes Miracles Still Possible
Isaiah 38:1–8

I want to tell you an awesome story from Isaiah 38:1–8. When King Hezekiah heard that he was going to die soon, he prayed to God desperately and asked Him to give him life. The Lord heard and answered his prayer, giving him fifteen more years to live. As a sign, the Lord made the sunlight step back ten steps.

Let me tell you one more story from the Old Testament, Joshua 10:12–14. Joshua and the entire Israelites' army marched all night to engage in war with Israel's enemies. Probably at dawn, they used a surprise tactic to attack the enemies. The Israelites' army was victorious, and the enemy, the Amorites, ran away. The Israelites chased them, but the sun was going down. Joshua then said to the Lord in the presence of Israel, "O sun, stand still over Gideon. O moon, stand over the valley of Aijalon." So, the sun stood still and the moon stopped until the nation of Israel avenged its enemies. In the historical record, the Book of Jashar, it was written, 'The sun stopped in the middle of the sky and delayed going down about a full day. There has never been a day like it before or since, a day when the Lord listened to a man.' " (Joshua 10:12–14)

Let us ponder for a minute to see how these phenomena happened. The sun rises in the east and moves toward the west, and this is always true, no matter where you live, because the Earth orbits the sun clockwise. This is a natural phenomenon that God arranged to make it possible for human beings to live stable lives according to an unchangeable time frame. It is a good thing that God created the concept of time to allow us to live according to a rhythm; variety and expectancy mysteriously work together in this time frame. Genesis 8:22 reads, "As long as the earth endures, seedtime and harvest, cold and heat, summer and winter, day and night will never cease." Time is the basic and essential fabric of every living creature's life span. As the sun continues to move from east to west, time passes and years go into the future; the future becomes the present as we age. Eventually, all of us will reach the end of our time, the end of our lives. Our time is in His hands, as Psalm 31:15a and 24 say: "My times are in your hands . . . be strong and take heart, all you who hope in the Lord."

Dr. Paul Tournier, a Swiss doctor, has a book called *The Seasons of Life*, in which he writes, "Sickness can suddenly overtake us at the very height of career and in the full frenzy of activity, with the same blow breaking it and, in some way, revealing it emptiness. Then it is that a man needs to find someone with whom he can talk about the problems besieging his mind."[29]

Each of our lives has its seasons, which may be compared to the seasons of the year. There is childhood—springtime; youth and young adulthood—exuberant summer season; the autumn of maturity and the winter of aging. Each of us is born into the world with the expectation of spending the whole year here and experiencing all its seasons. But some live only through the springtime, some enjoy the excitement of summer, some get to see the turning of the leaves in the mellow time; still others stay until the snow blankets the ground.

Hezekiah wanted to experience all the seasons of life, yet he didn't get the privilege to live a full life span. He had done great things for his country with his faith and his loving heart. He had experienced the season of blossoming; he overcame the hardships of life and had successes, and he became a famous and victorious king. Things were getting settled and stabilized. However, in his prime age, when he arrived at the time to enjoy peace after having passed through all his life's trials and storms, he faced death because of a severe disease.

All of a sudden, an unwelcome visitor knocked on his door: sickness and death. He cried out, "Now, Lord, you want me to be sick and die!" As you can see, Hezekiah was not just fearing death but also experiencing deep sorrow because he had to separate from his loved ones as you can read on Isaiah 38:11b, "No longer will I look on mankind, or be with those who now dwell in this world." Mankind and people who dwell with King Hezekiah were his loved ones and associates (author' interpretation)

---

[29] Paul Tournier, The Seasons of Life, translated by John Gilmour, (London: SCM Press, 1972), 46.

He felt a terrible sense of loss; he thought he had earned happiness and lovely people through his life's hard work, yet sickness and death were going to rob him of all of that: *"In the prime of my life* must I go through the gates of *death and be robbed of the rest of my years?"* I said, "I will not again see the Lord, the Lord, in the land of the living; no longer will I look on mankind, or be with those who now dwell in this world . . . like a weaver I have rolled up my life, and he has cut me off from the loom; day and night you made an end of me. I cried a swift or thrush, I moaned like a morning dove. My eyes grew weak as I looked to the heavens. I am troubled; O Lord . . . For the grave cannot praise you, death cannot sing your praise; those who go down to the pit cannot hope for your faithfulness" (Isaiah 38:10–11, 18, emphasis added).

He felt helpless. He could not find any strength in himself or his friends or from his power as king of a nation that had just been victorious against Assyria, the strongest country on those days. Nothing could help him.

So, this is what happened next:

- *Hezekiah desperately prayed to God.*
- *Hezekiah turned his face to the wall and prayed to the Lord. He wept bitterly, mourned like a dove, and cried like a swift or thrush (verse 14).*
- *The Lord answered his prayer; He saw his tears.*
- *Good news came to him; God's prophet, Isaiah, brought the message directly, "I have heard your prayer and seen your tears; I will add fifteen years to your life."*
- *A miracle happened. As the sunlight stepped back ten steps, God rearranged nature.*

With the amazing miracle of sunlight stepping back ten steps, God pushed time back only for one person, Hezekiah. God pushed the sun back to give fifteen more years of life for only one person, Hezekiah. This event was more amazing than if the sun had just stayed in place, as it had with the order of Joshua. I want you to imagine standing before the sun like Hercules and pushing the sun with all your strength. Can you move it an inch? Can you move it 0.00001 millimeters? No, nothing can happen with your power. But God did, with His mighty power; He pushed the sun one, two . . . ten steps back!

Now, guess what I want to discuss with this story? The miracles of God! Miracles impinge upon Christianity, and they are possible because of God's almighty power. We cannot be believers of the Bible or be Christians if we do not believe in miracles, because the Bible contains many stories of miracles from Genesis to Revelation.

The major pillars of our faith are based on the miracles of God: God's creation of the universe and human beings was a miracle.

The birth of Jesus Christ from the Virgin Mary was a miracle. Jesus' birth was not just difficult; it was impossible. Mary was a virgin. Only God could breathe life into her womb. And just as God caused her to conceive the perfect sinless Savior—fully God, fully human— He can accomplish, through you, those things that seem impossible in your life.

So much of God's redemptive history involves miracles that cannot be explained by human reason or natural law. The miracles prevail not only in the Old Testament but in the New Testament as well:

> Jesus fed more than five thousand with only two fish and five loaves of bread.
> Jesus Christ raised Lazarus from the dead.
> Jesus healed the man who was born blind.
> Most of all, He was raised from death and resurrected.

If we are not open to the possibility of miracles, we should delete many of the stories from the Bible. If we remove these stories, we deny the foundation of Christianity. Now, how do we define miracles? What is a miracle? Erickson's theology of "Miracle and Providence" gives answer to this question.

"Simply, it is a supernatural event, an unusual event that cannot be explained by common sense because it contradicts natural law. Water always should flow from up to down because of the law of gravity. When water goes up, it is a miracle. Let me tell you how miracles can occur. Miracles happen when supernatural forces counter natural forces. The laws of nature are not suspended; they continue to operate, but supernatural intervention negates their effects. Water can go up, even if the law of gravity continues to function, when the unseen hand of God is beneath the water. God simply could change the law of gravity, if it is His will.

If we are open to the possibility that there are realities and forces outside the system of nature, then why can't we believe that miracles are possible? Billy Graham said, "If we believe in the mighty power of God, why can't we believe—even if the Bible said that Jonah swallowed the whale!"[30] (author's paraphrase of Erickson' view on Miracle and God's Providence)

But our Christian view of a miracle goes a little further. A Miracle is a special supernatural work of God's providence that happens at the right time and at the right place to accomplish His divine purpose.

Erickson' view on the miracle is correct when he wrote, "Miracles happen when the people of God pray for help at the time of our need."[31] The importance of the miracle in Christianity is not whether it is supernatural or not, but it accomplishes God' sovereign will and provide His abound grace to us.

Durfee Martin wrote the hymnal, "Do not dismayed'. Betide" sang: 'Through days of toil when the heart doth fail, God will take care of you. When dangers fierce your path assail, God will take care of you. All you may need; He will provide; *God will take care of you; nothing you ask will be denied. God will take care of you*' (Durfee Martin, 1994, emphasis added).

Since God still performs miracles, it is our conviction that we are in the hands of a good, wise, and powerful God who will accomplish His will at the right time and in the right place to glorify Himself and to meet our needs.

More importantly, trust that God will give you victory over the terrible power of death; God raised Jesus from the grave with His almighty power and conquered the power of death for Hezekiah.

Trust God, who is almighty and powerful! Live a powerful life with the strength God gives you!

---

[30] Millard J. Erickson, Christian Theology, (Grand Rapids, Michigan: Baker Book House, 1983), 409.
[31] Ibid, 409-410.

For Reflection and Discussion

1. How does time control life? Discuss this in terms of the lives of King Hezekiah and Joshua (Isaiah 38:1–8, Joshua 10:12–14).
2. Think about the four seasons of life according to Dr. Paul Tournier's book, *The Seasons of Life*. What could you learn from Hezekiah's experience of deliverance from serious sickness and death, and what could you learn from his prayer?
3. What do you learn about God, who answered Hezekiah's prayer?
4. How did God give strength to the person who faced death and needed help desperately?
5. What is the miracle? What is the definition of a miracle in Christian faith?
6. Have you experienced a miracle in your life? Discuss it with your group. Give all attendees the opportunity to talk about their personal experiences with miracles.

God's Power Lifted up Elijah When He Was Depressed
1 Kings 18–19, James 5:17–18

> Then he prayed for rain, the heavens gave rain, and the earth produced its crops.
> —James 5:18, author's paraphrase

"There's one person whom I admire very much. I want to talk about him. I admire him because he has enormous strength—I mean he's bold, charismatic, and makes seemingly impossible things happen. Most of all, he is a very courageous man. He is my hero because I've always wanted to be like him. Do you know whom I am talking about? You may know him already. His name is Elijah."

There was a drought in Elijah's country for three and half years. His country's first industry is agriculture: rice, corn, and potatoes. Without rain people of Israel are dead; droughts cause food shortages. There was also an extreme shortage of drinking water. There was no way to take shower for three and half years. Can you imagine the smell of the sweat everywhere? In the extreme drought, there was one crazy man, Elijah, who thought he could ask God for rain. He prayed and prayed, but no rain. People thought that he was not in touch with reality. However, he constantly prayed. One day, there was a drop of water and a cloud the size of small boy's palm. Elijah believed that it was the sign that God was going to give rain. No one believed him. But all of sudden, it started to pour. Elijah's people were so glad that they got out of their houses and shouted for joy. From that time on, people have admired Elijah as a hero of the nation. Some of them would be so happy because they could take shower for the first time in three and a half years.

On another occasion, when everybody kept silent for fear of the evil king Ahab's revenge, Elijah alone stood up for the living God of Jehovah. He alone fought the battle with 850 false prophets and won.

Once, he raised a widow's son from the dead. On another occasion, when he prayed that it would not rain, it did not rain for three and half years. Elijah was a spiritual giant, and he was a very courageous man of God. Elijah was a legendary man.

However, there was an occasion when this spiritual giant was depressed. At first, it was hard to understand how this strong spiritual giant could possibly get depressed. More amazing, however, was that God uplifted Elijah in his time of depression and strengthened his life.

First, Lord fed Elijah physically.

All at once an angel touched Elijah and said, "Get up and eat." He looked around. There by his head was a cake of bread baked over hot coals and a jar of water. Elijah ate and drank and then lay down again. The angel of the Lord came back a second time and touched him and said, "Get up and eat, for the journey is too much for you. You still have a long way to go. You cannot give up here." So he got up, ate, and drank. Strengthened by the food that the Lord provided, he traveled forty days and forty nights until he reached to the mountain of God named Horeb. If Elijah lived in this century, he could have been the champion of Olympic marathoner like Abebe Bikila. In Rome, 1960, Ethiopian marathoner Abebe Bikila, running barefoot, became the first black African to take home a gold medal. Four years later in 1964, Abebea was the first man to successfully defend the marathon title.

There, on the mountain, Elijah went into a cave and spent the night. He was rejuvenated there. (1 Kings 19:5b–9, author's paraphrase)

As I watched how God uplifted Elijah, the first thing I learned was that food is so important to get over depression. I had seen some of my friends get depressed, and they denied themselves food. Their health deteriorated. They were getting down more and more until they got to the bottom of the pit. The cake of bread baked over hot coals was not mere food; it was food blessed with the love of God. Nutrition is so important to maintain our health and strength. Our health is important not just for our happiness but for carrying forth the mission that God gave to us. So, to get over the depression, you have to have good nutrition. Get up! Eat!

The second thing that amazed me was that God lifted Elijah up by showing him that he had many supporters around him. After the Lord strengthened Elijah physically, He counseled Elijah in order to sustain his emotional and spiritual life. The word of the Lord came to Elijah and said, "What are you doing here, Elijah?" Now, the Lord allowed Elijah to express his troubled mind; the Lord was ready to listen em-pathetically to Elijah's pain. Elijah talked to the Lord: "I have been very zealous for the Lord Almighty. But the Israelites rejected your covenant. I am the only one left. Not only that—they're trying to kill me now." Elijah was saying that his zeal for God's work was extremely strong; he had been working so hard for God. But he felt that there were no supporters who were with him. Elijah continued to say, "I am alone." This is a famous confession of Elijah's, known today as "Elijah's complex."

The first aspect of Elijah's complex is the feeling of rejection. Elijah worked hard without any recognition. He gave all his energy and risked his life for the Lord. But there was no appreciation or rewards; only rejection. Elijah said, "The Israelites have rejected your covenant." That meant that his fellow Israelites rejected Elijah too, which was why Elijah got depressed. It reminds me of what William James said: "The deepest of human desire is to be appreciated." Suffering was not the main cause of pain in this man's heart. A feeling of rejection and a lack of appreciation from his comrades were the major sources of pain for this spiritual giant.

The second aspect of Elijah's complex was the feeling of loneliness. It caused Elijah to become deeply depressed. Elijah said, "I am the only one left, and they are trying to kill me." He was thinking that he was the only one who suffered. "Why only me?" This feeling of loneliness made the spiritual giant even considers death. Loneliness is different from solitude. We all need quiet time, some solitude to spend with God alone. In solitude, we can sort out things and come up with new ideas and solutions. However, loneliness is not a healthy feeling. Elijah was a loner. He sojourned his life without friends. That was this spiritual giant's problem, and it was the cause of his complex. When I have seen strong and able men and women who reach the highest position without any help and stand alone at the top, I have admired them and their success has amazed me. However, when I have met them in their personal lives, I found that they were extremely lonely. They looked successful in their careers, but when they started to fall down, they ran down the hill very dramatically to the bottom of loneliness.

Have you been feeling like Elijah? If so, you are in Elijah's complex.

I've been there. The feeling of loneliness is a dreadful feeling.

I want you to know who has gone through this dreadful feeling of loneliness because I want you to know that you are not the only one who suffers this. First was Elijah, and then Jesus Christ our Lord suffered loneliness.

Jesus devoted His life to saving souls and caring for His people. However, when Jesus was very depressed, sweating blood because of His extreme stress and sorrow in the garden of Gethsemane, His disciples all slept. Jesus felt so lonely and asked them, "Can't you awake even an hour to be with Me?" Jesus performed so many miracles. He proved that He was from God, and He took care of His people dearly. Yet, when He hung on the cross, the words of His former followers lingered in His ear: "Crucify Jesus! Crucify Jesus!"

There seemingly was no appreciation, no recognition even, for the Son of God or Elijah. Only dreadful loneliness!

God lifted up Elijah as he confirmed to Elijah that he was not the only one who suffered. Listen to what God said to Elijah: "Yet I preserved seven thousand in Israel, all those whose knees did not bow to Baal" (1 Kings 19:18). Here, God was telling Elijah that he was surrounded by thousands of supporters: "You have comrades, 7,000 comrades who support you."

"Elijah, look around; I am with you, I am the sustainer who upholds you; I am your creator and the creator of the universe, the all-powerful and all-knowledgeable God. By the way, I am applauding you with clouds of witnesses, 7,000 comrades." This reminds me of Hebrews 12:1–3, which said, "Therefore, since we are surrounded by such a great cloud of witnesses . . . let us run with perseverance the race marked out for us. Let us fix our eyes on Jesus, the author and perfector of our faith, who for the joy set before him endured the cross, scorning its shame, and sat down at the right hand of the throne of God. Consider him who endured such opposition from sinful men, so that you will not grow weary and lose heart."

Some people who did not want an African to win the Olympic marathon competition put broken pieces of bottle on the way he was running, Abebe Bikila, running barefoot, still smiled, jumped over the pieces of broken bottles and kept on running because he fixed his eyes on the goal of crown. Finally, he got his crown.

Now, finally, God made Elijah stand in the presence of the Lord. God forced Elijah to rise above his depression. There, God uplifted Elijah by His gentle whispering voice. God showed three great events to Elijah; powerful winds that tore the mountains apart, an earthquake, and fire. But the word of God was not there. Sometimes, we look for God's comfort, presence, and signs from extraordinary events. Elijah also wanted to experience God in extraordinary events. However, God's presence and comfort were not in those events. This was quite a challenge to Elijah because he had previously experienced God in extraordinary events, such as when God brought fire from heaven to burn the altars of idols and when God gave rain miraculously. God's extraordinary feats caused Elijah to expect God's presence only in miracles. However, God's word was not there in the strong wind or the earthquake or the fire. God's presence on this occasion was revealed in an extraordinarily quiet way, in a gentle whispering. "After the earthquake came a fire, but the Lord was not in the fire. And after the fire came a gentle whisper" (1 Kings 19:12). God's presence

was revealed with that whispering. God whispered to Elijah, "Hello, hello . . . Can you hear Me? I love you; I care about you; I will take care of your country and its future."

Remember, God will uplift you spiritually when you quietly listen to Him. Christ taught at the Sermon of Mount, "Have quiet time in a closed room for your prayer, because God is listening when you have quiet time with God." The most important principle of prayer is quietly listening for the gentle whispering of the Lord. And you have to listen for God as attentively as when you take an Army hearing test: waiting, waiting for the slightest audible sound in one ear or the other. Focus on what God's whispering to your hearts! Hear what Jesus said: "I love you so much that I scarified my life to save you." Jesus rose for you to get into heaven eternally.

God lifted up Elijah in three steps: first, He give him nourishment: nice warm food and water; second, He made him aware that he had thousands of supporters and reminded him that he was not alone; and third, He spoke to his heart with a whispering voice. Knowing that God provides His strength in all areas of our lives—the physical, emotional, economical, and especially spiritual aspects of our lives—through His word, we just need to stand in His presence and listen quietly to His gentle whispering voice. Let me encourage you by reminding you that God will uphold you in whatever situation. He will give you strength to overcome problems.

For Reflection and Discussion

1. What is depression?
2. What cause it? Who could get depressed?
3. Talk about Elijah's experience with depression: what caused it, how it attacked, and how it made Elijah's life miserable.
4. Talk about how God lifted him up in three ways.
5. How could God lift up people who are depressed?
6. Meditate on the event in 1 Kings 18–19 and invite God to hear your heartache and lift you up.

One Changed person changed the World
Acts Chapter 9

A Boy Grown Up in a Tri-Cultured City

Saul was born sometime between 3–15 A.D. It was the period during which the Roman Empire started to blossom as a world superpower. Rome conquered the world and generally replaced Greek culture with their own, while simultaneously adopting parts of Hellenism into the fabric of society and culture. Jews were scattered around the world (Diaspora) for their survival and their land had been occupied and conquered by the Roman Empire. A Jewish boy named Saul was born during this time in Tarsus, the port city in the Mediterranean. Tarsus was set in the Cicilian plains. It had beautiful nature and cultured buildings, universities, and temples.[32] The merchants, philosophers, and rich travelers gathered at Tarsus to pursue their business, debate, and enjoy life. Saul's parents were wealthy enough that they could buy Roman citizenship. Although he was a Jew, Saul was born as a free Roman citizen. Growing up, Saul was exposed to three cultures: Hellenism, Rome's empiricism, and the Jewish traditional pious culture. He was exposed to the polytheism that was part of port city life, similar to modern San Francisco.

Saul's parents who were strict and pious Jews who raised their son as a traditional Jewish boy. Saul was a genius and grew up as an outstanding Pharisee among Pharisees. Saul was groomed as a prominent young scholar who mastered all three cultures. He knew the power of Rome, the brilliance of Greek knowledge, and the spirit of Judaism. He still remained as a patriotic traditional Jew, however, who wanted to see his country become a powerful nation in his lifetime.

---

[32] Henrietta Buckmaster, A Man Who Changed the World (New York: McGraw-Hill Book Company, 1965), 5.

Saul Encountered Jesus

To Saul, the Nazarene who claimed to be the Messiah was quite an unpleasant figure. Jesus' teachings countered Saul's fierce loyalty to Judaism. Jesus' teaching of blessings was contrary to Saul's idea of blessing: "Blessed are those who are poor, blessed are those who mourn, blessed are those who are meek . . ." To Saul, Jesus' teachings did not fit at all within Judaism.

Jesus was so influential; however, that soon he had many followers. Even Rabbis came to him. Young and old, women and men, fishermen and CPAs followed Jesus. Because of Jesus' popularity and his performance of miracles, Zealots watched him and wanted to know if he would overturn Rome to become a delivering Messiah. But Jesus had not come to raise a sword. Instead, he said, "My kingdom is not of this world."

Eventually, Judaism could not accept what they saw as blasphemous teachings, and they appealed to Rome to execute Jesus on the cross, which was the symbol of curse. There had been two thousand criminals crucified in the place where Jesus' cross stood. People thought that one righteous man who had stood against worldly power had died and was gone. But soon Jesus' disciples proclaimed that Christ had been resurrected and spread the Gospel powerfully. Jesus' resurrection threatened the authority of Judaism even more than his life. Saul was zealous for Judaism and called himself a Hebrew of the Hebrews, from the tribe of Benjamin, the cornerstone of the Pharisees. He believed that Judaism made him righteous and blameless. He felt that the Christians were challenging the holy position of their Messiah and blaspheming the Hebrew tradition.

Stephen, one of Christ's followers, known as a man who some theorize came from the same city as Saul, stood one day among a Jewish crowd and delivered a powerful and persuasive speech. With a perfect knowledge of Jewish history and Judaism, Stephen claimed that Jesus was the Messiah. This man was too dangerous for the Jews, and in their fear and anger, they stoned Stephen to death. Saul plotted to get rid of Stephen. The first witnesses against Stephen dragged him out of the city in order to topple him over a cliff. They wanted to show their mercy when they stoned a criminal by putting him on a cliff and pushing them off for a quick death instead of prolonging his pain. Instead, scripture says that the crowd stoned him to death, taking off their outer garments during the process, and laying them at Saul's feet.

If both Stephen and Saul were from same city of Tarsus, Stephen could have been a classmate of Saul when they were young. They could have shared their dream of a Messianic kingdom when they were adolescents. Assuming that they were close friends before, Stephen could not have felt more betrayed. Saul, seeing Stephen's cruel death, thought that he had done the right thing for his tribal religion.

As the stones broke Stephen's body, however, they also may have broken the hard heart of this young zealot. When he heard the Stephen's prayer, "Lord Jesus, receive my spirit. Lord, do not hold this sin against them," he surely remembered that it was the same prayer Jesus had prayed on the cross, a prayer for the forgiveness of the persecutors. He must have wondered, "How could Jesus and Stephen pray for their enemies during the most extremely painful and shameful moment of their lives?"

Saul's Eye-Opening Experience

Saul was passionate about the law and desired to meet the Jewish Messiah; he yearned for the truth. Instead, he ended up as a cruel killer of innocent witnesses of Christ and still did not realize humankind's predicament. He was blind to the true light. God came into this man's life unexpectedly; it was an act of total grace and God's initiated intervention. A sudden light made this spiritually blinded man's eyes physically blind, and then God spoke to Saul directly with his voice:

Saul, Saul, why persecutest thou me?
Who art thou, Lord?
I am Jesus whom thou persecutest.
Lord, what wilt thou have me to do?
Arise, and go into the city, and it shall be told thee what thou must do.
(Acts 9:4-6, AV)

When Saul stood up, the brilliant light so filled in his eyes that he could not see. It was an irony to blind the eyes of Saul who was blind spiritually. It was a physical misery, but it was the way that God wanted to bless Saul—he opened Saul's spiritual eyes through this painful experience. God sent Saul a true helper, Ananias. It was miracle that God visited Saul who persecuted Christ. It was a miracle that God brought Ananias to the persecutor Saul to guide and open his spiritual eyes. As the scales fell from Saul's eyes and his vision cleared, the vague hope of laws faded out from his heart. His spiritual eyes became absolutely clear; he was able to see the truth clearly. When Saul heard from Ananias, "Brother Saul," he remembered Stephen's prayer, "Forgive; do not lay the sin to them." When he remembered the voice of Jesus, "Why are you persecuting me? I am calling you as my vessel," he wondered why Jesus would call a persecutor like him. He had never experienced such a great compassionate love throughout his life. It opened his eyes to the real God's love, and to his new hope in the true Messiah, Jesus Christ.

Paul's Change Changed the World

Once Saul the rebel, zealot, and persecutor had been transformed into a servant, this changed vessel of God began to spread the Messiah-ship of Jesus Christ. Saul who became Paul changed the world. Before Paul started to work for the Lord, he went to desert to discover God in a deeper way. Below Damascus lay the Arabian Desert and it stretched all the way to south Sinai and, to the East, the Euphrates. He could have stayed there for forty days or three years. Compared to the city Tarsus in which he grew up, this Arabian Desert offered nothing to comfort him. There were no cultured structures, no temples, no synagogue, and no library. There was only sun and loneliness, the sand, and that was all![33] Why did Paul choose the Arabian Desert to find himself and God? History does not tell the answer. It was clear, however, that his experience in the desert was similar with Jesus Christ's self-discovery in the wilderness.

The changed man, Paul, became a man who changed world history. He explored every city in the world in his journey to change people's lives with the Gospel, the good news of redemption, hope for the mankind. I want to remind you one transformed person, could affect the reform of the world, with the story of Martin Luther King Jr.

---

[33] Buckmaster, Henrietta Paul, A Man Who Changed the World, (McGraw-Hill Book Company, 1965) 25.

Dr. Martin Luther King, Jr. and James Earl Ray-

The unimaginable cruelty of racism and injustice were prevalent in the days of Dr. Martin Luther King, Jr. Blacks could not ride on the same bus with white men. There was severe inequality and segregation of the people. King stood up so that God's justice could change America. One incident from his life follows:

> The garbage men were paid $1.70 an hour. The loss of six hours' pay meant $ 10.20 . . . The strike couldn't last. After all, $1.70 an hour was above the national minimum. The garbage men were ready to accept. But money was not the issue. Race was.[34]

Circumstances impact people's life either positively or negatively. Especially when hardship comes to their lives, each responds differently. So, trial is a good tester of each character. Trials visited both King and James Earl Ray, albeit in different situations and forms. One responded positively and contributed greatly to people's lives. One responded negatively and assassinated the great man, King. One became the assassinated Reverend, champion of non-violence. One became assassinator, promoter of violence. There could be no way to compare these two men other than the contrast of darkness and light.

One description of the assassinator follows:

> In prison, convicts made sport of James Earl Ray. They called him "hard luck character," "stupo," a natural loser in the field of crime. Sometimes, walking the cobbles in the prison yard, he opened his mouth to say that when he got out he was going to make one "big lick." He was in and out of prison so frequently that some wardens referred to James Earl Ray as the "commuter."[35]

---

[34] Jim Bishop, The Days of Martin Luther King, Jr. (New York: G.P. Putnam's Sons, 1971), 486.

[35] Bishop, The Days of Martin Luther King, Jr., (New York: G.P. Putnam's Sons, 1971) 40.

King suffered imprisonment in order to defend justice. Yet he always led non-violence movements for justice; he was always in the front of the march. While King was in jail, another "outsider" arrived in Selma. The tall, cavernous figure of Malcolm X walked on Broad Street. The word passed that "Malcolm is here, right here in Selma," and it frightened more blacks than whites. Malcolm X spoke of violence as though it were inevitable and good. Malcolm impressed King, who wanted to visit with him while in jail, because King sought to harmonize justice and peace together.[36]

People were frightened and screaming when King was assassinated.

People felt that it was like the end of daylight, according to Bishop:

There was a cracking sound like two flat boards being slapped together. The bullet traveled at 2,600 feet per second. The Reverend Martin Luther King, Jr., neither heard anything nor felt anything. "The bullet hit Dr. King a half inch below the right side of his hip, shattered his jaw, severing the spinal cord. Death, in such cases, is almost instantaneous; the heart may fight to continue its functions, but a broken spinal cord, in addition to shock, is its own anesthetic. In the courtyard, someone began to moan, 'Lord, Lord!' Andrew Young and Bernard Lee were now at his side. 'Oh, God, it's awful,' Young said. 'It's all over.' An empty shell casing fell in the bathtub and rolled around the bottom. Surely, James Earl Ray must have been pleased. Once, just once, he had carried out an assignment correctly. The time in Atlanta was an hour later: 7:13 P. M. The phone rang. It was Jesse Jackson. "Coretta," he said, "Doc's been shot." "Now the savior was gone, and it was more than a husband. It was a mentor; a Christian teacher of love, a hater of hate, a man who fought by keeping his hands down and accepting the blows of his enemies—the good man was gone."[37]

It was like the day when Cain killed his brother, Abel, unjustly shedding his blood. He still spoke, however, even though he was dead (Heb. 10:4). As the Lord said, "Abel's blood cried out to God from the ground." Although King died, his voice of "Let Justice roll on like a river, righteousness like a never failing stream!" kept on ringing in people's minds.

It seemed as if King knew how he was going to die, although he did not know when it would happen. He said, "I don't know what will happen now.

---

[36] Ibid., 180.
[37] Bishop, The Days of Martin Luther King, Jr., 167-168.

We have got difficult days ahead. But it doesn't matter to me because I have been to the mountaintop. Like anyone else, I would like to live a long life. But I'm not concerned with that. I just want to do God's will, and He has allowed me to go up the mountain. I see the Promised Land. I am happy tonight that I am not worried about anything. I do not fear any man. Mine eyes have seen the glory."[38] He was like Moses who saw the vision of the Promised Land, but did not have an opportunity to enter in. He had a vision and dream, but he did not live to see them fulfilled.

Dream Speech and the Joyous Day of Victory

King delivered his famous dream speech, a good portion of which follows:

> I say to you today, my friend, that in spite of the difficulties and frustrations of the moment I still have a dream. It is a dream deeply rooted in the American dream. I have a dream that one day this nation will rise up and live out the true meaning of its creed: "We hold these truths to be self-evident; that all men are created equal." I have a dream that one day on the red hills of Georgia the sons of former slaves and the sons of former slave owners will be able to sit down together at the table of brotherhood . . . Let freedom ring; when we let it ring from every village and every hamlet, from every state and every city, we will be able to speed up that day when all of God's children, black men and white men, Jews and Gentiles, Protestant and Catholics, will be able to join hands and sing in the words of the old Negro spiritual, "Free at last! Thank God Almighty, we are free at last!"[39]

King's dream speech was definitely a diamond among all sermons that ever have been preached and it became an inspiration for decades since, swaying people's hearts.

---

[38] Ibid., 360.

[39] Bishop, The Days of Martin Luther King, Jr., 380.

John F. Kennedy, President during King's time, welcomed the march of Negroes after King's dream speech. He actually was enthusiastic to King's movement, and stated, "We have witnessed today in Washington thousands of Americans—both Negro and white—exercising their right to assemble peacefully and direct the widest possible attention to a great national issue."[40]

It did not take long for America to listen King's voice. His dream was for all Americans, as he believed, "I know you are asking today, 'How long will it take?' I come to say to you this afternoon, however difficult the moment, however frustrating the hour, it will not be long, because truth pressed to earth will rise again."[41]

Martin Luther King was a strong Christian who had a desire to follow God's will, not just in the pulpit proclaiming the Gospel of salvation, but also at the time when he marched for the justice of God with his people. Both Paul, who changed the world with the proclamation of the Gospel for saving souls, and Dr. Martin Luther King Jr., who followed God's will for justice, were changed men who changed the world. It was possible because of Christ's Agape love that was expressed on his cross, "Forgive these men who crucify me, their sin because they do not know what they are doing." Both Paul and Martin Luther's life story gives us hope because Agape love can change the person and the world into a peaceful loving global community although there are still injustice, hate in this human society.

---

[40] Ibid., 384.
[41] Excerpt from Dr. King's speech that ended the march on Selma on March 25, 1965.

CHAPTER 7

HOPEFUL LIFE

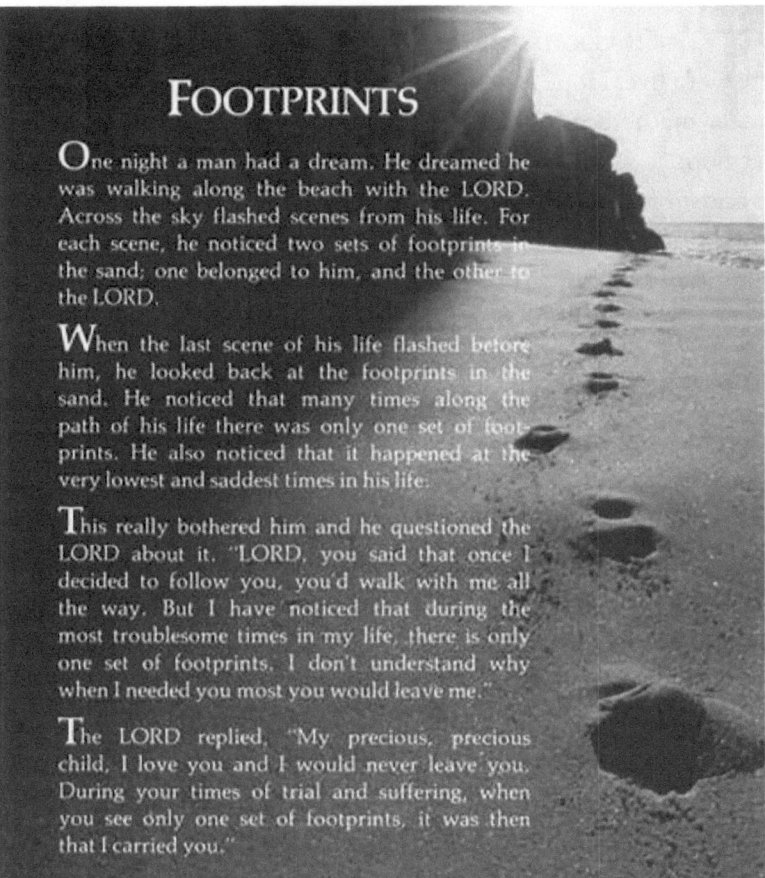

FOOTPRINTS

One night a man had a dream. He dreamed he was walking along the beach with the LORD. Across the sky flashed scenes from his life. For each scene, he noticed two sets of footprints in the sand; one belonged to him, and the other to the LORD.

When the last scene of his life flashed before him, he looked back at the footprints in the sand. He noticed that many times along the path of his life there was only one set of footprints. He also noticed that it happened at the very lowest and saddest times in his life.

This really bothered him and he questioned the LORD about it. "LORD, you said that once I decided to follow you, you'd walk with me all the way. But I have noticed that during the most troublesome times in my life, there is only one set of footprints. I don't understand why when I needed you most you would leave me."

The LORD replied, "My precious, precious child, I love you and I would never leave you. During your times of trial and suffering, when you see only one set of footprints, it was then that I carried you."

If You have Hope, Wait Patiently
Romans 8:24–25, 1 Kings 18:41–46

> For in this hope we were saved. But hope that is seen is no hope at all. Who hopes for what he already has? But if we hope for what we do not yet have, we wait for it patiently.
> —Romans 8:24–25

HOPE IS VERY IMPORTANT TO US; it motivates us and gives a reason to live. Hope is neither just wishing something to happen nor the method of victory.

Yet hope is solid for those who have faith; it gives us a purpose to live in the midst of suffering. Hope is the ability to see a positive future even in times of darkness. It reconstructs our lives even after failure, moves us beyond our iniquities toward maturity and success. Most of all, it gives us the vital energy to overcome life's disappointments and frustrations; we can rejoice even when we fail and feel the unfairness of life.

Let me tell a story about one man, Viktor E. Frankl, who survived the Holocaust, Nazi death camp at Auschwitz. He was the weakest person in the prisoner's camp, and he was not intelligent. There was a healthy and strong man in the same camp; there also was a very smart person. Everyone thought that the strongest or the smartest would survive. Strangely enough, the weakest person survived. It was because he always held the hope that he would someday be united with his family, his lovely wife and children.

Harold S. Kushner, Ribbi emeritus @ Tempe Israel in MA, USA wrote the forward message in the book of Viktor E. Frankl, *Man's Searching for Meaning*. In that forward message, he told the amazing Viktor's story of the survival because of the hope he held: "Who had lost all hope for a future were inevitably the first to die. They died less from lack of food or medicine than from lack of hope, lacking of something to live for. By contrast, kept himself alive and kept hope live by summoning up thought of his wife and the prospect of seeing her again, and by dreaming of lecturing."[42]

On the wall of the deep dungeon of the Jewish Holocaust camp, someone found amazing scribbled, which said, "It is so dark here, and I cannot see the sunlight. However, I believe that the sun rose today, because I know that there is a sun still running around the universe."

I read about a person who found the hope that brought the light in her life in the midst of darkness when she went through the horrible persecution at Jewish holocaust camp:

> "Every single day at some point I see that archway etched vividly in my mind's eye. I try to come to terms with all that I feel and the dark horror of those dreadful days engulfs me and drags me back there to the wartime abyss of death that is still Auswitch.
>
> Darkness shrinks from the smallest light. A small candle can be seen from afar in the darkness. More than sixty years ago a small flame was lit in the dark of man's bestiality when he abandoned his God. That light still burns as brightly today. I look at Ruth and she lights up my dark places.
>
> Ruth is a daughter of the Holocaust, a true light in the dark."[43]

The one essence of the hope that God gives us is eternity, which is neither visible nor attainable in the moment: "But hope that is seen is no hope at all. Who hopes for what he already has?" (Romans 8: 24 b, NIV) Therefore, real hope is something that you cannot see at the moment yet are able to grasp in your mind and heart. What hopes can we grasp?

Salvation.

The eternal kingdom of God in heaven.

Paul used a strong argument: "For this hope we were saved, and who hopes for what he already has?" He used a contradicting concept for salvation: "We are saved in the past tense already," but, added, "we do not have complete

---

[42] Viktor E. Frankl, Man's Searching for Meaning, (Boston, MA: Wilsted & Taylor Publishing Services, 1959), edition. Beacon press 2006, 9-10.

[43] A Light in the Dark - Personal Holocaust - The Jewish Magazine, March 2010 Edition www.jewishmag.com/142mag/holocaust.../holocaust_experience.htm (accessed on August 30, 2011)

salvation in our hands yet."(Author' Interpretation of Romans 8:23) It seemed that Paul was contradicting the concept of salvation and confusing the issue. Was he talking about two different things? No.

Hope connects the past and the future.

Romans 8:22–24 says the obvious reality that everyone goes through groaning, even those who are saved already.

"We know that the whole creation has been groaning as in the pains of childbirth right up to the present time. Not only so, but we ourselves, who have the first fruits of the Spirit, groan inwardly as we wait eagerly for our adoption to sonship, the redemption of our bodies. For in this hope we were saved". (Romans 8:22-24a)

When I do ministry at the hospital, I see, hear, and even smell groaning, pains. Sometimes, their pain is unimaginable to ordinary healthy people.

There are horrible catastrophes of nature and war in these modern days: hurricanes, the 9/11 attacks, the Haiti earthquake, the China earthquake, the Chile earthquake, and so on.

Groaning.

Pain.

Hopelessness.

Despair.

We thought we were getting into the pain-free zone since we became Christians. That is true in some sense. However, children of God are not immune to the groaning and pain. Pain visits even those who have the first fruits of the Spirit. People who have the first fruits of the Spirit are those who have experienced the joy of salvation. Saved! You might think that they would at least not have to struggle with temptation or sin. When people are saved, they enter a spiritual honeymoon and are joyful for a while. However, when that first period of their salvation experience passes, they again are tempted and groan inwardly. They might wonder what happened to their salvation.

Are these kinds of struggles familiar to you? This is an honesty check. You can answer to yourselves.

Even Paul, who could be called a true saint, struggled and groaned inwardly when he was in the highest stage of the matured Christian's life: "In my inner being I delight in God's law; but I see another law at work in the members of my body, waging war against the law of my mind and making me a prisoner of the law of sin at work within my members. What a wretched man I am! Who will rescue me from the body of death?" (Romans 7:22–24) He felt such despair and was so hopeless.

In spite of the hopelessness that we might feel about the reality of everyone's sinfulness and the imperfect world, we still could grasp the hope that we will be completely free from sin in the future when God resurrects our whole beings as spiritual bodies.(Interpretation of 1st Corinthians Chapter 15: 36-49)

We are saved in the realm of eternity; the hope of our salvation looks toward, in its essence, eternity.

But we still struggle in this imperfect world within the boundaries of our imperfect bodies. That is why we yearn for the days of eternity and complete redemption. Everything in the world—the beauty, wealth, fame, and even good health—changes and fades away. "All men are like grass and all their glory is like the flowers of the field. The grass withers and the flowers fall, but the word of our God stands forever" (Isaiah 40:6–8). Therefore, the ground of our eternal hope does not belong to this world. Our true hope is eternal salvation and the forever kingdom in heaven. Hope for eternity will not disappoint you. Your stance will not change and shatter according to circumstances; it will last forever and satisfy your souls. It will not shatter even when your stock's value goes down.

Do you feel hopeless when you look around the world, realize your circumstances, and see the terrible things happening?

Pray that God would give you hope; pray that the Holy Spirit would breathe hope into your heart. God will not disappoint you, because the hope God gives you is the eternal hope that the Spirit breathes in your heart; it is the hope that God will fulfill His promises.

The second essence of hope is that it will become your vital energy to see the bright future in times of difficulty: "But if we hope for what we do not yet have, we wait for it patiently" (Romans 8:25).

Hope is in the future. With hope, you can grip the future as a real thing, and it will enable you to wait happily and patiently. It will give you strength to overcome frustration and have success. You will have a joyful harvest eventually; you will be like Paul, the faithful marathoner who can laugh with the abundant happiness at the last moment when he finish the course. II Timothy 4:7-8a "I have fought the good fight, I have finished the race, I have kept the faith. Now there is in store for me the crown of righteousness."

According to 1 Kings 18:41–46 and James 5:17–18, a prayer in faith can bring great results because God hears our prayers. Importantly, this can give us hope even when everything seems like it is falling down. "Elijah was a man just like us. He prayed earnestly that it would not rain, and it did not rain on the land for three and half years. Again he prayed, and the heavens gave rain, and the earth produced its crop" (James 5: 17–18).

1 Kings 18:41–46 is an excellent and sacred story of hope.

Attempting something three times is not as easy as it seems. After failing once and then maybe a second time, many people will give up. But there will be some who will try a third time and experience the victory and joy of success.

However, here Elijah tried seven times. Nothing happened the first six times, but in the seventh time the Lord showed just a little sign: a small cloud the size of a man's hand. Who could hope that that small cloud would bring heavy rain to quench the thirst of those people who had suffered in the drought for three and a half years? Elijah did.

We, the believers in God, are people who can see gracious and abundant rains coming from a small sign, a cloud as small as a hand.

Do not say that there is nothing; say *I cannot see yet, but it is coming.*

Even when you only see a 0.001 percent chance of something happening, you can say that it is coming and achieve your hope. The greatness of Thomas Edison was not just inventing the electric light but of his faith in the time there seemed no possible solution. You should see the hope even in the small clouds, and you should try the things you want to achieve at least seven times.

When Thomas Edison invented the light bulbs, he tried over 2000 experiments before he got it to work. A young reporter asked him how it felt to fail so many times. Edison said, 'I never failed once. It just happened to be 2,000 step process.'

Trust and believe that God will pour His gracious rain on you and bless you abundantly, even when you see just a very small sign.

God's blessing is stored in heaven for you.

Galatians 6:9 says, "Let us not become weary in doing good, for at the proper time we will reap a harvest if we do not give up."

In due time, you will experience the joy of the harvest, and your life will be fruitful. God will eventually bless you.

For Reflection and Discussion

1. What is hope? What is eternal hope?
2. What does hope do to people?
3. Do you ever feel hopeless as you look around the world and realize the terrible things happening? What is the hope that God gives you?
4. Discuss Elijah's hope when he could not see any clue for how to find a solution. What kind of hope was that? How could he have had hope when everything was falling apart?
5. When does hope become reality? What do we need to do to see our hope actualized in real life?

Living Faith, Living Hope
Hebrews 1:1–3, 11:6; Colossians 1:15–20

Since the spring is visiting us and the trees are starting to get green these days, I would like to talk about how the leaves are able to sustain their green color. The roots pull water and nourishment from the ground and send it to the leaves. Can you guess how much power it takes to pull one drop of water to the leaves at the top of trees? For some of the leaves on the top of red cedar trees in northern California, it takes twelve horsepower for one drop of water to make the journey!

We enjoy seeing the amazing natural changes and balances throughout the four seasons: spring, summer, autumn, and winter. How beautiful those are! How are the seasons possible? God created the four seasons, as first mentioned in Genesis 8:22: "As long as the earth endures, seeding and harvest, cold and heat, summer and winter, day and night will never cease." These seasonal changes started when Noah's flood was over. Before the flood, the earth had a perfect and consistent temperature. Living things existed in amazing living conditions, which made it possible for human beings to live healthy and very long lives; some lived over 700 years; some, 969 years. After the flood judgment, God showed His grace with the rainbow promise. Soon after God showed the rainbow, He started giving us the beautiful and well-balanced seasons. Genesis 8:22 explains it very well.

Scientifically, the seasonal changes were possible because God shifted the earth a little bit and tilted it at a slight angle, 23.5 degrees.

The Living God Upholds You

Who runs nature? Someone might say, "It is simply a natural phenomenon." Someone else will say, "Once He created it, God let nature run itself."

However, Hebrews 1:3 says that the universe continues to run because Jesus Christ, the Son of God, sustains it: "The Son is the radiance of God's glory and the exact representation of his being, sustaining all things by his powerful word. After he had provided the purification for sins, he sat down at the right hand of Majesty in heaven." The word *sustaining* was translated in the Revised Standard Version as *upholding*.

Therefore, Christ, along with God the Father and the Holy Spirit, sustains and upholds the universe and your life from alpha to omega. Colossians 1 says the same truth: "He is the image of the invisible God, the firstborn over all creation. For by him all things were created: things in heaven and on earth, visible and invisible, whether thrones or powers or rulers or authorities; all things were created by him and for him. He is before all things, and in him all things hold together" (Colossians 1:15–17). The concept of creation repeated is three times in these verses and *emphasizes Jesus as the creator*.

The concept of Christ as the creator with God the Father echoes the first verse of Genesis and the gospel of John: "In the beginning God created the heavens and the earth" (Genesis 1:1). "In the beginning was the Word, and the Word was with God, and the Word was God. He was with God in the beginning. Through him all things were made; without him nothing was made that has been made" (John 1:1–3). The phrase "In the beginning" and the verb "created" share the same word root that means continuing creation. In the Hebrew language, the noun describes not just existing things but also moving objects. So, although "beginning" is the noun, it tells about God the Father and the Son of God creating the universe and continuing to do the work of creation that sustains the universe.

I once visited the Ardennes Memorial Cemetery in Belgium for a Memorial Day ceremony. There, I read the inscription on the monument. Three words caught my attention: *supported, provided,* and *maintained*. To win the war and sustain, the troops had to be provided and supported. The essential condition for winning the war was to make sure there was a supply route. If supporting and sustaining forces were not behind them, although the Allied forces were strong, they could not win the war. That same principle applies in life and in the universe. God continuously supplies and sustains His power to uphold the universe and life.

Now, let us imagine that the electricity and the water supply stops in your area. All of the sudden, the electricity goes off and the lights go off as a result! Have you experienced that? One winter, hot water didn't come out for a few hours, and I had to take a cold shower in the morning. It was not so pleasant.

Now, continue to imagine that the sun stops shining and the earth stops rotating around the sun. Since we see the sun rising every morning, we assume that the sun will rise again tomorrow morning. We assume that the universe will continue to run smoothly without any effort. We assume that we will breathe tomorrow and continue to live. However, without Christ's sustaining power, this universe and our lives will not move an inch and the sun will stop shining.

If fact, such things happened for six hours when Christ was dying on the cross. Christ prophesized that there will be a repetition of this catastrophe when He comes back: "The sun will be darkened and the moon will not give its light; the stars will fall down from the sky, and the heavenly bodies will be shaken. At that time men will see the Son of Man coming in clouds with great power and glory." (Mark 13:26-27)

Now, do you realize how much energy and effort are required to keep us breathing, the green leaves green, and the sun shining? The energy that the sun gives in a second is more than all the energy that human beings have used in all of history, and God is sustaining all of these powers. It takes lots of energy and effort to sustain all of these things.

One good example is the heart contraction. Psalmist, with his amazement for the awesomeness of God's creation of the human five organs and six parts in-most beings of human body sang, "For you created my inmost being; you knit me together in my mother's womb. I praise you because I am fearfully and wonderfully made; your works are wonderful, I know that full well. My frame was not hidden from you when I was made in the secret place. When I was woven together in the depths of the earth." (Psalms 139: 13-15)

The average human being's pulse is about 72 per second. So, in a day—24hrs times 60 minutes times 60 seconds,—a person heart jumps approximately 6220,800 times. Doing push- up or sit-up exercise 50 times a day is already a good work- out per day and the muscle already tied up. Yet the heart muscle, membrane, is not tired of jumping the heart when it jumps 6220,800 times a day and it continues on our whole life.

That is how God wonderfully created the human body, especially the heart.

I am amazed about how God created human' inmost being and intrigued and so I include researches about the heart muscle and its contraction.

Cardiac Muscle is a very specialized tissue that has both the ability to contract and the ability to conduct electrical impulses. Muscles are classified both functionally as either voluntary or involuntary and structurally as either striated or smooth. From this, there emerges three types of muscles: smooth involuntary (smooth) muscle, striated voluntary (skeletal) muscle and striated involuntary (cardiac) muscle. The names in the brackets are the common names given to the particular classification of muscle.[44]

Cardiac muscle is a type of involuntary striated muscle found in the walls and histologic foundation of the heart, specifically the myocardium. Cardiac muscle is one of three major types of muscle, the others being skeletal and smooth muscle. The cells that comprise cardiac muscle, called myocardiocyteal muscle cells, are mononuclear, like smooth muscle cells.[1]

Coordinated contractions of cardiac muscle cells in the heart propel blood out of the atria and ventricles to the blood vessels of the left/body/systemic and right/lungs/pulmonary circulatory systems. This complex of actions makes up the systole of the heart.

Cardiac muscle cells, like all tissues in the body, rely on an ample blood supply to deliver oxygen and nutrients and to remove waste products such as carbon dioxide. The coronary arteries fulfill this function.[45]

Cardiac muscle is adapted to be highly resistant to fatigue: it has a large number of mitochondria, enabling continuous aerobic respiration via oxidative phosphorylation, numerous myoglobins (oxygen-storing pigment) and a good blood supply, which provides nutrients and oxygen. The heart is so tuned to aerobic metabolism that it is unable to pump sufficiently in ischaemic conditions. At basal metabolic rates, about 1% of energy is derived from anaerobic metabolism. This can increase to 10% under moderately hypoxic conditions, but, under more severe hypoxic conditions, not enough energy can be liberated by lactate production to sustain ventricular contractions.[46]

---

[44] Sandra K. Ackerley (ackerley@uoguelph.ca), Department of Zoology, University of Guelph, Guelph, Ontario, Canada N1G 2W1 (accessed on August 18, 2011).

[45] University of Guelph Developmental Biology ONLINE! web site (retrieved 2010-05-04) http://www.uoguelph.ca/zoology/devobio/210labs/muscle1.html (From Wikipedia, the free encyclopedia) (accessed on August18, 2011).

[46] Ganong, *Review of Medical Physiology*, 22nd Edition. Specialized form of muscle that is peculiar to the vertebrate heart, p81 (From Wikipedia, the free encyclopedia

Here is another excerpt about an amazing natural phenomenon: how we can be on a spaceship, Earth, which moves 29.78 kilometers a second, yet still survive without becoming dizzy.

Considering the Earth-Moon system as a binary planet, their mutual center of gravity is within the Earth, about 4624 km from its center or 72.6% of its radius. This center of gravity remains in line towards the Moon as the Earth completes its diurnal rotation. It is this mutual center of gravity which defines the path of the Earth-Moon system in solar orbit. Consequently the Earth's center veers inside and outside the orbital path during each synodic month as the Moon moves in the opposite direction. The Moon's orbital path around the Sun (accompanying the Earth in its own path around the Sun) is always convex outwards.

Unlike most other moons in the solar system, the trajectory of the Moon is very similar to that of the Earth. The Sun's gravitational pull on the Moon is over twice as great as the Earth's pull on the Moon; consequently, the Moon's trajectory is always convex (as seen when looking inward at the entire Moon/Earth/Sun system from a great distance off), and is nowhere concave (from the perspective just mentioned) or looped.

If the gravitational attraction of the Sun could be "turned off" while maintaining the Earth-Moon gravitational attraction, the Moon would continue to orbit the Earth once every sidereal month.[47]

Psalm 139:13–15, Isaiah 44:24 and Isaiah 64:8 say that God is the Creator of our mysterious lives and the universe.

When I think about all of these natural phenomena, I am amazed by how big and powerful our God is! More amazingly, God wants to share His power with us and uplift us! Christ not only sustains and upholds the universe, He upholds and sustains you because He cares about and loves you. He even cares about the condition of the wallet in your pocket. Jesus is not just upholding you spiritually but also emotionally, physically, and economically. Therefore, I can sing a song:

I can face tomorrow because He lives. All fear is gone
Because He holds my future,
And life is worth a living just because He lives.

(accessed on August 18, 2011).

[47] http://en.wikipedia.org/wiki/Orbit_of_the_Moon (accessed on February11, 2011).

God Wants to Give You a Reward

Our loving Almighty God wants to give us a reward because He wants to give us joy. Faith is not just believing in the mightiness of His power and His existence, but putting our trust in God that He would reward us. Hebrews 11:6 says, "And without faith it is impossible to please God because anyone who comes to him must believe that he exists and that he rewards those who earnestly seek him."

There are many people who deny the existence of God, yet many of them live lives that have nothing to do with God. Those are the Existential Theists. Those who do not trust God to give them a reward are actually the same as non-believers.

Jesus said that God is the "God of Abraham, Isaac, and Jacob." He also revealed Himself as Jacob's personal God: "I am Jacob's Almighty God." He is the God of living persons, a personal God of "I and Thou," not "I and it." (As the Martin Buber defines the personal relationship with God and us, not like the relation with the objective that has no feeling and thought)

Our living God creates, motivates, moves, guides, and inspires us. He leads our lives with His sovereignty. He jumps our heart, balances the seasons of the year, counts our hairs, provides our food, and protects us from harm. He is the Lord of our lives (Psalm 139:13–15; Isaiah 44:24, 64:8).

Do you want to please God? If you do, believe that He not only exists but also gives you rewards.

If my son did not expect me to supply something that he needed, it would make me sad. Don't you know that God would feel this even more than the earthly father who wants to give good things to his children? Jesus said very positively, "Ask and it will be given to you; seek and you will find; knock and the door will be open to you" (Matthew 7:7).

Therefore, earnestly seek His graceful reward, hope for the reward, believe in the reward, and get the reward.

For Reflection and Discussion

1. What is your view about the creation of the universe?
2. Look at the amazing natural phenomena around you, especially the lives of human beings and our earth's environment, which perfectly supports life. Discuss how God, who arranges all of these natural principles, operates in the universe and our lives.
3. Meditate on Hebrews 1:3, Psalm 139:13–15, Isaiah 44:24, and Isaiah 64:8, and think about God, who is living and sustaining life.
4. Meditate on Hebrews 11:6 and answer, "How can we have a faith that pleases God?"

I Will Glorify You
Romans 8:29–39

"And those he predestined, he also called; those he called, he also justified; those he justified, he also glorified" (Romans 8:30).

The promise of Romans 8:30 gives us a hope. God promised that He would ultimately lead our lives and take us to the highest stage of glorification.

Ultimately, God gets the only glorification. Yet He wants to put you in the seat next to Him to share the glorification, just as a father wants to have his children next to him to share the privilege of the father. The purpose is neither for our self-glory nor to promote vain pride but for our inward beautification.

Romans 8:30 explains the three steps of the pilgrimage: calling, become righteous, and glorification. God guides those whom He predestined. God's providence advances us in those three stages of life, finally making us ready to reach glorification.

I would like to talk about these three stages through Abraham's pilgrimage through life.

Calling

God called Abram, who lived in Haran and was originally from Ur, in two ways: He commanded Abram to leave his current life, and He made him a promise.

First God said, "Leave your country, your people and your father's household and go to the land I will show you." Second, God promised, "I will make you into a great nation and I will bless you; I will make your name great, and you will be a blessing. I will bless those who bless you, and whoever curses you I will curse; and all peoples on earth will be blessed through you."

First of all, the source of God's calling is His divine will; we do not originate it.

Jesus told His disciples, "I called you as friends. I chose you to bear fruit; you did not choose Me" (John 15:16, author's paraphrase). It is hard to understand the concept of predestination. Didn't Andrew and Peter follow Christ and choose to be with Him? Didn't we choose the way of God voluntarily? Of course we did! Peter and Andrew also chose to follow Jesus with their will. However, God predestined these choices. God planned, led, and inspired us to follow His way of life.

Callings come from high, and so it is a grace of God that we become His children. Romans 9:15 talks about the sovereignty of God's calling. "For He said to Moses, 'I will have mercy on whom I have mercy, and I will have compassion on whom I have compassion.'"

What's the purpose of God's calling, and what is required of us to respond to His calling?

God's promise to Abraham gave a dream to an ordinary person. Abraham had a good life at Haran. However, he did not have a dream in his life. His name means an honored father, yet he childless when he was seventy-four years old. What irony. I have a friend whose last name is Smallwood. He is six-foot-five-inches tall. People address this very tall boy, "Hi, Smallwood." People addressed Abraham, this childless elder, "Hi, exalted father." Whenever people addressed Abram, it would have reminded him that he was an old man who was childless and therefore had no dream, who just lived an unproductive and meaningless everyday life just like a squirrel circling in a cage.

Do you just live a repetitive daily life without meaning or dreams, moving from one day to another? God wants you to have big dreams. God's promise to you contains a big dream: "I will make you a great nation."

Another of God's purposes in calling us is to bless us as we become the source of blessing. God promised: "I will make you into a great nation and I will bless you; I will make your name great, and you will be a blessing. I will bless those who bless you, and whoever curses you I will curse; and all peoples on earth will be blessed through you."

What does the blessing mean to you? It would mean different things depending on each person's perspective. To a person who struggles for good health, good health is a blessing. To a person who struggles with marriage, a good and happy marriage is a blessing. Good health, a happy marriage, both of those are blessings. What would you say if I asked you to list five of your blessings? Healthy teeth, a long life, good children, wealth, and a happy family could be blessings. The Old Testament and New Testament use two different languages, Hebrew and Greek, but each language's word for *blessing* means exactly the same thing.

Blessing means happiness.

The purpose of God's calling is to bless us and gives us real happiness, yet it goes further; it blesses us to become a source of blessing to others. Our blessings are meant to contribute to our blessing others. God calls us to become people who would give joy and laughter to those who are depressed and sad, hope to those who despair, strength to those who are weak, and peace to those who have anxiety. Blessing others really makes us happy too.

What is the purpose of God's calling us? It is to bless others. Everyone wants to be blessed, yet God's people want to share their blessings with others; we want to receive blessings in order to bless others. It is like a well that we dig out to feed all the people in the village.

Abram got the calling from God when he was in the village of Haran, yet he was originally from Ur. Ur, in about 3000 BC, was the most developed city in the world and the origin of Mesopotamian culture, which was one of the four original cultures of the world. It was later developed as the ancient Babylonian empire. They already used bronze; it was the middle of the Bronze Ages. Although Ur was an advanced and cultured city, they worshipped idols, especially the bull. An ancient bull-worshipping temple still exists in that area.

Ur was located east of Euphrates River. When God called Abram, he had to leave his country, hometown, and kin. To leave his hometown, he had to cross the Euphrates River. The first essence of being called is leaving one's hometown and people. To follow the calling and go to the Promised Land, Abram left Ur and crossed the river. So, Abram's descendants were called Hebrews, which means "the people who crossed the river" (Joshua 24: 2–3, 14; Genesis 31:19–35:52).

Therefore, the prerequisite for following God's calling is leaving one's comfort zone. We want to stay in our comfort zones because we feel safe and are familiar with everything that surrounds us; we feel cozy and happy. There is nothing wrong with stay in in our comfort zone. But to follow our dreams, to advance, sometimes we are required to leave our comfort zones.

A calling is a departure from one's old life. Please, do not misunderstand that everyone has to leave her loved ones and hometown. Leaving one's family to start a faith pilgrimage brings chaos, and that practice breaks families.

The purpose of leaving one's family and hometown in Abram's day was to get away from idol worshipping. The principle at hand is that we must depart from old habits, bad relationships, and idols to have a new start.

Abram should have felt lonely in his life journey because he left his kin. Some of us crossed the Pacific Ocean to come to America. I sometimes feel homesick and miss my kin in Korea.

Was it not possible for Abram to serve God in Ur? Why did he have to suffer emotionally and leave his people? Were there ways that he could have kept his old lifestyle and served God?

No.

To start a new life, you have to leave your old life. Jesus said, "Only new wine skin can keep new wine." Starting of a new life means leaving! Being called requires—mandates—leaving. May God reveal things, people, habits, lifestyles, and cultures that you have to leave to follow His calling and start a blessed new life!

God called Abram out of Ur and sent him to the Promised Land so that he could single-heartedly follow Him. Abram became so close to God that God even called him a friend. God was not ashamed to be known as the personal God of Abram, Isaac, and Jacob. God wanted to be known as the mighty Jehovah God of Abram. That was the privilege of God's covenant people. Those who discover the greatness of privilege of God's calling us as covenant people will be overwhelmed like David who was so thankful when he discovered the Almighty God's mindfulness to him. (Psalm 8:4).

Romans 8:15–17 says, "The Spirit you received does not make you slaves, so that you live in fear again; rather, the Spirit you received brought about your adoption to sonship. And by him we cry, 'Abba, Father.' The Spirit himself testifies with our spirit that we are God's children. Now if we are children, then we are heirs—heirs of God and co-heirs with Christ, if indeed we share in his sufferings in order that we may also share in his glory."

The relation with God to us is not I and it, but I and You (Thou) since we call Him as Abba Father and inherit His glorious Kingdom.

Justification: Righteousness

God called Abram when he was seventy-five years old, and He promised that he would become a great nation with many descendants. It had been ten years, yet still Abram did not have any children. God gave Abram a great vision, but Abram did not have a lot of ambition. He just wanted to have a son. He did not ask for any big favors from God; he just wanted to become an ordinary father who had a son. A decade passed, and he still could not see any sign of children. He could have given up on his dream. He could have regretted following God and believing in His promise. He could have felt that he had followed a vain rainbow of a dream. Abram said to God, "O Sovereign Lord, what can you give me since I remain childless? You have given me no children." What was God's response? He took Abram outside his tent and said, "Look at the heavens and count the stars—if indeed you can count them." Then He said to him, "So shall your offspring be." It was a moment when Abram could have replied, "Lord, just give me a son. I do not ask for many children like the countless numbers of stars in heaven; just one. I have waited enough. How much longer should I have to wait?" But Abram didn't question God's promise. Rather, he put his complete and total trust in the Lord's promise.

The Bible simply states, "Abram believed the Lord." Believed! Abram believed! Abram believed the Lord! Abram did not offer any fancy words or beautiful statements; nor did he present a profound philosophy. All we know is that one word of trust.

His belief totally depends on the "promise"; there were no signs to support it. He trusted the One who promised him. That was all he needed to do, and that was all he could do; that was all God wanted from Abram.

And God credited Abram's belief to him as righteousness.

Now, Abram reached the stage of righteousness in his faith pilgrimage: those he called, he also justified (Romans 8:29). This stage of justification is not similar to the ethical progress of human beings. You do good deeds, you earn righteousness; that is what human morals and ethics say. In other religions and other values, you have to earn ethical and religious righteousness, and therefore righteousness is an achievement. You work hard to get it, you pay a lot to get it, and you deserve to have it. However, the righteousness that God gives His people is totally different. It's righteousness that we could only get from His favor and grace.

It was very hard to understand the concept of righteousness for those who just believed. To those who worked hard to become righteous, especially those who followed the Law of Moses and lived ethical lives, it was unacceptable.

The concept of God crediting our righteousness was hard to understand for the son who worked hard to earn his father's love in the parable of the prodigal son (Luke 15). Paul explained the concept of grace in Romans 4:1–3: "What then shall we say that Abraham, our forefather according to the flesh, discovered in this matter? If, in fact, Abraham was justified by works, he had something to boast about—but not before God. What does Scripture say? 'Abraham believed God, and it was credited to him as righteousness.'" That is the truth that God illuminated to the hearts of Paul and Martin Luther. The Holy Spirit inspired them with of the idea, "The righteous shall live by faith."

God gives us righteousness not because He wants to degrade the ethical or moral aspects of life, but because God knows that human beings could never reach the standard of His righteousness. "For all have sinned and fall short of the glory of God, and all are justified freely by his grace through the redemption that came by Christ Jesus" (Romans 3:23–24).

Martin Luther, who was born in 1483, tried hard to become a righteous person in the dark ages of Christianity, and he became a monk. One of ways that people in his day thought they could become righteous was through self-discipline and self-restriction; they could overcome their sinful desires by climbing up Pilate's stairs in the cathedral in Rome with bare feet and bare knees. He thought that he could become free from sin by condemning the sinful body, yet as he tried harder to punish his sinfulness, he became more desperate. In response to Luther's honest and long quest, God gave a surprising answer to Luther. One day the Spirit gave him an illumination with the words of Romans 1:17: "The righteous shall live by faith":

"Luther came to the conclusion that the "justice of God" does not refer, as he had been taught, to the punishment of sinners. It means rather that the "justice" or "righteousness" of the righteous is not their own, but God's. The righteousness of God is that which is given to those who live by faith. It is given, not because they are righteous, nor because they fulfill the demands of divine justice, but simply because God wishes to give it. Luther tells us, "I felt that I had been born anew and that the gates of heaven had been opened. The phrase 'the justice of God' no longer filled me with hatred, but rather became unspeakably sweet by virtue of a great love."[48]

---

[48] Gonzalez, Justo L, *"The Story of Christianity," The Early Church to the Present Day*, (Peabody, MA: Prince Press, 2009), 15-16.

Luke 15 gives us the best explanation of the grace that enables us to get this righteousness.

The grace of God was what made the prodigal son righteous— nothing the son did made him so.

Glorification

> Those he justified, he also glorified.
> —Romans 8: 30

The saint's final stage is glorification; it could be the stage of sanctification: those He justified, He also glorified. Those He justified, He also glorified! This is the basis of our confidence in the preservation of our salvation, in our irrevocable calling from God. Once God calls, He guarantees that He will help us reach the highest stage of sanctification and glorification. He is sincere. Job looked for to become glorified when he was painfully suffering; he said "After all of these trials, I will come out like fine gold." (Job 23: 10b)

God's promise has two sides: glory that is outward and inward humble character.

Inward glorification means that our characters would resemble Christ's image: "For those God foreknew he also predestined to be conformed to the likeness of his Son, that he might be he firstborn among many children" (Romans 8:29). Our inner beings, our characters, will become more like Christ: loving, kind, generous, holy, and wise.

Outward glorification means that our position becomes honored; *He will lift us up and highly exult us.* Mary, Jesus' mother, praised the Lord when God foretold that the coming Messiah would come from her womb: "He has performed mighty deeds with his arm; he has scattered those who are proud in their inmost thoughts. He has brought down rulers from their thrones *but has lifted up the humble*" (Luke 1:51–52, emphasis added). Isaiah prophesied the glorification of the suffering servant in the future: "See, my servant will act wisely; *he will be raised and lifted up and highly exalted*" (Isaiah 52:13, emphasis added). God highly exalted Joseph, as He gave him the position of Egypt's prime minister. God gave him glory so that he could save the world from starvation. Joseph said in a testimony of his faith, "You intended to harm me, but God intended it for good to accomplish what is now being done, the saving of many lived" (Genesis 50:20).

God's promise to Abram became actualized with the glorification of his fourth descendant, Joseph. This was God's fulfillment of His promise throughout the generations. Joseph became a person who could feed the world in a time of world recession. It foretold that his seed, Jesus Christ, would bless all nations and give salvation to the world. Abraham, Isaac, Jacob, and Joseph were all used in this great redemptive history. Just as God honored Joseph and Abraham, He will honor you when He uses you in His great redemptive history.

For Reflection and Discussion

1. What are the three stages of the faith journey? What do Romans 8:30 and Abraham's life journey tell about these stages? What faith stage are you at now in your spiritual journey?
2. What was the purpose of God calling Abram?
3. Why did God ask Abram to leave his old life to follow the calling? What does God's calling on Abram say about His calling on you?
4. What was the difficult situation that Abram faced in Genesis 14 and 15?
   Meditate on Romans chapter 4:1–3 and on Abram's faith in Genesis 15:5–6.

5. What do you learn about faith in Romans 4:1–15 and Genesis 15:5–6? What does faith do? How one could become righteous? (Also see Romans 1:16–17.)
6. What was Martin Luther's spiritual enlightenment, and how did it reform Christianity and affect history? (Romans 1:16–17.)
7. How did God give righteousness to the prodigal son? Discuss how God makes humankind righteous.
8. How has God glorified you?
9. What are two aspects of glorification?
10. Meditate on the Scripture, "And those he predestined, he also called; those he called, he also justified; those he justified, he also glorified" (Romans 8:30).

The Highway to Heaven Is Wide Open
Genesis 28:12, John 1:50–51

When Jacob was a teenager, he had to flee to his uncle's house to escape from his twin brother Esau's rage. Jacob never had left his parents' house before. He ran and ran, trying to get away as far away from his avenger as possible. Once he was tired and could not go further, he stopped at a place named Bethel. As a matter of fact, he was the first person who named that place *Bethel*. The place Jacob arrived that night was actually called as, "Nowhere". When Jacob arrived there, he did not know where he was. He was like a lost sheep. He did not know what was ahead of him in his near future. He was lonely, fearful, and anxious about the uncertainty of tomorrow. Depression fell upon him. Finally, he became sleepy. In the wilderness, he found one stone and used it as a pillow. He laid his head on it and slept in the wilderness.

Whenever I go on a field, my first item to put in the duffle bag is my pillow. It is soft and very flexible, although it doesn't look great. That is my minimum comfort in the field time. But Jacob had only a cold and rigid stone pillow, which tells us that Jacob was going through a very tough moment. Even worse, he felt he had been cut off from his relationship to God and his family, his mother, father, brother.

When Jacob slept, God appeared in his dream and promised that He would be with him, protect him from any danger, bless and bring him back to his home. It was the promise of Immanuel: God's presence, protection, and guidance for this poor boy.

"I am with you and will watch over you wherever you go, and I will bring you back to this land. I will not leave you until I have done what I have promised you."

It was quite a surprise to Jacob because he thought that God' presence was only in his Parent' Jacob and Rebecca's tent. He found out the Omnipresence of God; God who is with him even in the wilderness. He was amazed for the presence of God in the wilderness. He was overwhelmed with the fact that God was with him in his most desperate moment. He said, "Wow, Surely the Lord is in this place." So, when he woke up early in the morning, He took a stone that he used as his pillow on last night and set it up straight to use as the pillar, the altar for the worship. And he named that place as, "Bethel", which means, 'house of God.'

It was only a stone he picked up in the wilderness, but since he found the God's presence with him there first worshiped God in his life, Bethel was the most meaning place.

Then, Jacob saw an amazing scene in his dream: "He had a dream in which he saw a stairway resting on the earth, with its top reaching to heaven, and the angels of God were ascending and descending on it" (Genesis 28:10–22). God showed him a big bridge (stairway) that reached heaven.

What is a ladder or stairway for?

It is a vertical bridge that connects the earth to the top of the roof, a place we can't reach by ourselves. I want you to now picture Jacob's dream of the ladder. I will show this artful and beautiful picture of Jacob's dream.

Fear, anxiety, uncertainty about the future, and separation from loved ones! Those experiences and feelings could be compared with the earth; they were Jacob's earth. As God showed him the stairway to heaven and angels on the bridge who were descending and ascending on it, God was showing him that *He* would carry him to heaven, which meant that God would carry Jacob to hope, joy, and—most of all—to eternity. Jacob did not know what the bridge-ladder meant at the time. No one knew what the bridge (stairway) in Jacob's dream signified until Jesus broke the code. When Jesus started His ministry, He said, "I tell you the truth, you shall see heaven open and the angels of God ascending and descending on the Son of Man" (John 1:51). John 1:51 is the pairing Scripture with Genesis 28:12, which describes Jacob's dream.

The "Son of Man" refers to Jesus Christ, who had left the comforts of heaven to come down to be with human beings. Jesus was showing us that He would become our bridge to heaven. Angels of God will take us to heaven safely if we just stay on the bridge of Jesus Christ.

I would like to show the famous Golden Gate Bridge and the old prison, named Alcatraz Island, in Bay area.⁴⁹

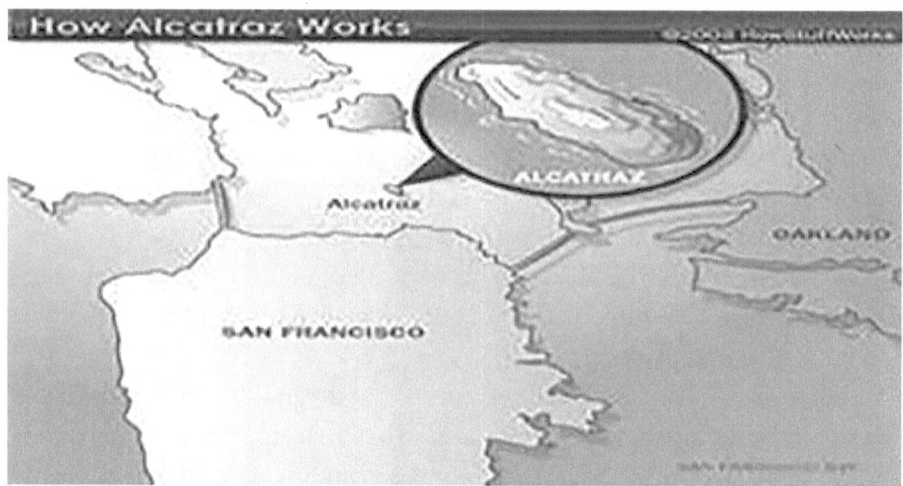

The federal prison on Alcatraz Island in the chilly waters of California's San Francisco Bay housed some of America's most difficult and dangerous felons during its years of operation from 1934 to 1963. Among those who served time at the maximum-security facility were the notorious gangster Al "Scarface" Capone (1899-1947) and murderer Robert "Birdman of Alcatraz"

---

⁴⁹   https:/www.google.com/search Alcatraz map (Accessed on Jan 12. 2017)

Stroud (1890-1963). No inmate ever successfully escaped The Rock, as the prison was nicknamed, although more than a dozen known attempts were made over the years. After the prison was shut down due to high operating costs, the island was occupied for almost two years, starting in 1969, by a group of Native- American activists. Today, historic Alcatraz Island, which was also the site of a U.S. military prison from the late 1850s to 1933, is a popular tourist destination. Whether or not anyone succeeded in escaping from Alcatraz depends on the definition of "successful escape." Is it getting out of the cellhouse, reaching the water, making it to land, or reaching land and not getting caught? Officially, no one ever succeeded in escaping from Alcatraz, although to this day there are five prisoners listed as "missing and presumed drowned."[50]

Nowadays, you can cross the San-Francisco Bay easily and safely by driving on the San-Francisco Bridge, just in 20 minutes.

I am showing this to explain the separation of the human being from God as the metaphor and the necessity for the bridge to cross over from this earth to heaven.

There is a great chasm between heaven and us. The river of death, the force of evil, and sinful human nature block us from heaven.

We are like people who stand before the bridge and cannot return; yearn to return yet could never do go back; they sorrowfully separated from God. People also suffer separation among themselves because of wars and hostilities between nations and tribes.

In Genesis, the Lord God banished Adam and Eve from the beautiful garden. After they were driven out, God placed cherubim and a flaming sword flashing back and forth on the east side of the garden. Why? He did this to guard the way to the Tree of Life. Adam and Eve could never come back to Eden. The sword of God's judgment stood between fallen human beings and God's garden. It separated human beings from God, keeping human beings from ever returning to Paradise.

---

[50] https:/www.bop.gov/about/history/Alcatraz.jsp

One of Jesus' parables in Luke 16:19–31 illustrates the separation between human beings and God. The rich man and the beggar named Lazarus both died. When the beggar died, the angels carried him to Abraham's side. The rich man also died and was buried. He went to Hades, the place of deep darkness. In Hades, where he was in tormented, he looked up and saw Abraham far away with Lazarus by his side. So he called to him, "Father Abraham, have pity on me and send Lazarus to dip the tip of his finger in water to cool my tongue, because I am in agony in this fire." But Abraham replied, "Son, remember that in your lifetime you received good things, while Lazarus received bad things. However, now he is comforted here, and you are in agony. And besides all of this, a great chasm has been fixed between you and us" (Luke 16:19–31, author's paraphrase). The fiery and deep chasm was fixed between heaven and Hades.

There was no bridge between heaven and earth. Not even an old, rotten, small bridge was laid between God's realm and Hades. Only a great chasm was fixed there.

If God did not provide Christ as a bridge to Him, we would all be separated from Him and would have no way to return to paradise.

Without Christ, we would be like people standing before a great chasm and yearning to cross over but unable to do so.

The good news, however, is that Christ became our bridge to God.

He became our bridge to eternity and to joyful life in His kingdom.

Luther experienced that Jesus could give him the righteousness of God and the freedom of the spirit. Furthermore, Martin Luther found that Christ was the only ladder that could enable him to reach heaven. I would like to tell the story of Luther's conversion experience. His father was a peasant and wanted to grow his son, Luther as the lawyer who had a power and good social status. His father was so strict and disciplined him a lot. In those days, they were allowed to whip the kids. His father many times whipped Luther, not evil purpose, but to push him to become a knowledgeable lawyer. Although he knew the purpose of his father's strict discipline, he was always fearful of his father and even hated him. When Luther became the Monk of the Catholic, he went through the same experience of punishing himself and discipline of Catholic law. As one way of pilgrim Journey, he had to crawl and went up to the Altar through many steps of St. Peter's Church with the bear knee as a way to punish his sinful body and to become righteous person. To him, God was same like his strict father, fearful. He could never experience the peach with God. One day, Martin Luther learned from Romans 1:17 that the righteous comes only by faith. He learned that Christ suffering on the cross and his redemption make it fully possible for Luther became righteous: It is given, not from punishment of his sinful body and keeping strict law of Catholic, only by faith of Jesus Christ and make him complete righteous person. He said that he felt like to see the heaven was open for him and had a peace with God and peace with him the first time in his life. This conversion experience became the epoch of the new Christian movement, which started the Protestant Church.

We do not want to be blocked from the happiness in heaven. So, we try to cross the river with our own effort. But as Martin Luther learned from Romans 1:17: our efforts do not make us become righteous. The righteous shall live only by faith, and Christ is the only way to heaven.

Without Christ, we are like the prisoner in the Alcatraz Island that could not escape the rapid and chilly waters of the Bay area of San-Francisco.

Without Christ, we are like Jacob with his head on the cold stone pillow.

Without Christ, we are like the rich man who died and asked only for a dip of water but couldn't cross over that great chasm to reach Abraham's side.

We all belong to this earth, hopelessly separated from God just as Adam and Eve were blocked from the Garden of Eden by the sword of flame. However, the good news is that Christ became our bridge to heaven, to the garden of happiness, and to our loving God. All we need to do is get on His Bridge, and then the angels of God ascending and descending will carry us to heaven. The highway to heaven is open wide, and Christ will carry us there.

Just as Jesus became a bridge for Luther and Jacob to reach heaven, Jesus will become our bridge to heaven. Now, we can cross over the river of death, sin, despair, hopelessness, and sadness and reach heaven.

It is my prayer for you today that you would get on this big ladder, the Son of Man, Jesus Christ, the highway to heaven.

Lord, now, we come to realize that we fall short of the glory of God. With our own effort, we could not reach to the righteous. We are not at peace with you or with our neighbor. We have troubled minds and want to have peace with you and peace in our hearts. Now we are accepting Jesus Christ as our reconciler, the bridge to You. Bless all of us as we get on the bridge of Jesus Christ to reach heaven. In Jesus' name, we pray.

For Reflection and Discussion

Principle One

God loves you forever and wants to give you a perfect and happy life.

Principle Two

Despite God's abundant love and blessings for us, humankind fell in the garden of Eden.

John 1:50–51 is the pairing verse with Genesis 28:12. What do these Scriptures say about humankind's dilemmas and the solutions for them?

Read the story in Genesis 3:22–24 about the exile of humankind from Eden, and read the parable in Luke 16:19–31 about the rich man and the beggar Lazarus. Discuss humankind's dilemmas.

What was Martin Luther's struggle?

Principle Three

What truth saved Martin Luther from his struggle and gave him the experience of peace and of heaven being wide open?

Who is Jesus Christ in the story of Genesis 28:12 and in the Scripture of John 1:50–51?

How does Jesus reconcile us with God and humankind?

Principle Four

Christ as the bridge to heaven that reconciles you with God. Experience the salvation, heavenly joy, and hope in the promise of God's kingdom.

Christ's Coming Back: Hope for the Generations

1 Thessalonians 4:13–18, 5: 1–11; Matthew 24:26–27, 30, 37; 25:1–13

This subject may be foreign to some people, and they may say, "There are plenty of things to worry about today, and I do not want this foreign subject in my life." However, let me tell you that the promise of His return is very good news, because it is a message of hope.

The Bible, in 1st Thessalonians 4:13–18 and 5: 11, discusses the return of Jesus Christ: "Brothers, we do not want you to be ignorant about those who fall asleep, or to grieve like the rest of men, who have no hope . . . Therefore encourage each other with these words . . . Therefore encourage one another and build each other up" (author's paraphrase).

Three words stand out from this passage, and those words are very familiar in these days of turmoil: *grief* and *no hope*.

What are antidotes of these? Encourage one another, and build each other up.

The Pauline Epistles start and end with the encouragement of hope. They also explain the basis of the Christian hope, which is in Christ return. Encourage, encourage! There is a lot of discouraging news these days, yet the message of Christ's return is encouraging news.

When Jennie, one of my congregants, died, I visited her husband. I just stayed with him, because I could not find any word of consolation. Facing the sudden death of his loved one, he said, "Do not say anything to comfort me; if you can, just bring her back."

One way or another, everyone experiences the grief and sorrow that comes from the death of a loved one. We want to say a word of consolation to those suffering such loss. However, it is hard to find the right words. When the United States experienced the great tragedy of the attack on the World Trade Center in New York on September 11, 2001, there was chaos, disaster, anger, cruelty, and especially hopelessness because of all the death and the fact that people were separated from their loved ones. There was no way to give consolation, and many became hopeless.

However, the message of eternity and life in heaven gives us hope. You can count on Christ coming back. You can expect His word to come true, and you can live a hopeful life because of this hope and faith in eternity.

When we talk about "The second coming of Jesus Christ," there are four important questions we might ask or be asked: Are you sure He is coming back? When will His return be? What will His second coming look like? How do we get ready to meet Him?

The Sureness of the Second Coming of Christ: Matthew 24–25, Acts 1:9–11, John 14, Revelation 22:7–21

Let me start by answering the first question: "Do you truly believe Christ's coming back?" To some people, it is the matter of interpretation. But actually, it is the matter of either belief or unbelief. If we believe that Scripture is trustworthy, we will believe in the second coming of Jesus Christ. Christ's promise and prophesy about His second coming are trustworthy because of the sincerity of God's promise. I will lay out here what Jesus and the Holy Christian Scripture say about His coming back.

In His great discourse in Matthew 24 and 25, Jesus promised that He would come again: "Then will appear the sign of the Son of Man in heaven. And then all the peoples of the earth will mourn when they see the Son of Man coming on the clouds of heaven, with power and great glory" (Matthew 24:30).

When Jesus was standing before Caiaphas for the hearing, He declared, "But I say to all of you: From now on you will see the Son of Man sitting at the right hand of the Mighty One and coming on the clouds of heaven" (Matthew 26:64).

In John 14, Jesus continually tried to convince His disciples of the sureness of His second coming: "I'm going away; you can't follow Me there." As they heard this, the disciples worried about their future. They asked, "Lord, why can't I follow You now?" "Lord, we don't know where You are going, so how can we know the way?" "Lord, show me the Father." Jesus promised them that He was coming back and said, "In my Father's house are many rooms. I am going there to prepare a place for you; I will come back and take you to be with Me so that you also may be where I am. I'm going away, but I am coming back to you" (author's paraphrase).

The book of Acts records the promise of His return: "After he said this, he was taken up before their very eyes, and a cloud hid him from their sight. They were looking intently up into the sky as he was going, when suddenly two men dressed in white stood beside them. 'Men of Galilee,' they said, 'why do you stand here looking into the sky? This same Jesus, who has been taken from you into heaven, will come back in the same way you have seen him go into heaven'" (Acts 1:9–11).

The Revelation of John starts with a greeting that indicates Christ's coming back: "Grace and peace to you from him who is, and who was, and who is to come" and ends with the strong confirmation of Christ's coming back, "He who testifies to these things says, 'Yes, I am coming soon.'" John responded, "Come, Lord Jesus" (Revelation 1:4, 22:20).

We can trust His word as truth because of the sincerity of His promise. God always keeps His promises. The first coming of the Messiah was prophesied in the Old Testament from Genesis through David, Isaiah, and Jeremiah. Prophecies of the Old Testament focused on the coming Messiah, and God fulfilled all of those prophecies. Therefore, we can be sure of the coming fulfillment of the prophesied second coming of Jesus Christ.

The Signs of Christ's Return and the Features of His Second Coming

Many people ask questions like the ones the disciples asked Jesus: "When will this happen? What will be the sign of Your coming?"

Instead of answering them about the date and time of His return, Jesus emphasized the suddenness of the coming of the Son of Man: "As it was in the days of Noah, so it will be at the coming of the Son of Man" (Matthew 24:37).

In 1 Thessalonians 5:1–3, the Bible echoes what Jesus said about the suddenness of His return: "Now, brothers and sisters, about times and dates we do not need to write to you, for you know very well that the day of the Lord will come like a thief in the night. While people are saying, 'Peace and safety,' destruction will come on them suddenly, as labor pains on a pregnant woman, and they will not escape."

There are dangers in trying to find the precise date of His return, because false prophets can trap you. Jesus warned, "So if anyone tells you, 'There he is, out in the wilderness,' do not go out; or, 'Here he is, in the inner rooms,' do not believe it. For as lightening that comes from the east is visible even in the west, so will be the coming of the Son of Man" (Matthew 24:26–27).

Signs of Christ's Return

Do you remember the remarkable day of the history that caused of the end of World War II? Invasion of Normandy (D-Day), Operation Overlord, during World War II, Operation Neptune began on D-Day (June 6, 1944) and ended on 30 June 1944. D-day came as a sign that ends the war.[51]

Just like that, there will be signs when it is near the day of Christ's return.

Jesus said that many world catastrophes would come first as signs of the nearness of His coming. He said,

> There will be signs in the sun, moon and stars. On the earth, nations will be in anguish and perplexity at the roaring and tossing of the sea" (Luke 21:25).

"The day of the Lord" in the Old Testament is the sign of the nearness of the last days of this world, and it gives the perfect picture of the second coming of Christ. "Let all who live in the land tremble, for the day of the Lord is coming. It is close at hand-a day of darkness and gloom, a day of blackness." (Joel 2:1-2) The day of the Lord in the Old Testament is same as the day of Christ's second coming. Jesus said that on the last day, "people will faint from terror, apprehensive of what is coming on the world, for the heavenly bodies will be shaken. At that time they will see the Son of Man coming in a cloud with power and great glory. When these things begin to take place, stand up and lift up your heads, because your redemption is drawing near" (Luke 21:26–28). Jesus said that the last day would be the dreadful Day of Judgment and that it would come suddenly like a thief in the night. The message of His return is not a sweet message, because the day of terrifying judgment will come prior of Christ's return. Jesus even asked

---

[51] Normandy Landing, en.wikipedia.org/wiki/Normandy_landings (accessed on 29 August, 2011).

His disciples to pray that it might not come in the winter, because it would be very difficult to endure.

The contrast between Jesus' First Coming and His Second Coming

What will Jesus look like at His second coming?

The features of Jesus Christ's return will not be like those of His first coming. Jesus humbly came in a lowly manger as a baby when He first came down to earth. His return will sharply contrast with the first coming. He will come on clouds with great power and magnificent glory. At that time, the sign of the Son of Man will appear in the sky, and all the nations of the earth will mourn, because Jesus will come as the judge of the universe. He will be accompanied by His angels and heralded by archangels. He will sit upon His glorious throne and judge all the nations. Clearly, He will be the triumphant, glorious Lord of all (Matthew 24:30–31). "For the Lord himself will come down from heaven, with a loud command, with the voice of the archangel and with the trumpet call of God" (1 Thessalonians 4:16).

The Apostle John also described his second coming in the book of Revelation. He wrote,

> "Then I saw heaven opened, and behold, a white horse. And He who sat on him was called faithful and true, and in righteousness He judges and makes war. His eyes were like a flame of fire, and on His Head were many crowns. He had a name written that no one knew except Himself. He was clothed with robe dipped in blood, and His name is called The Word of God. And the armies in heaven, clothed in fine linen, white and clean, followed Him on white horses. Now out of His mouth goes a sharp sword, that with it He should strike the nations. And he Himself will rule them with a rod of iron. He himself treads the winepress of the fierceness and wrath of Almighty God. And He has on His robe and on His thigh a name written "King of Kings and Lord of Lords." (Revelation 19:11–16)

The Second Coming of Jesus Christ Is the Message of Hope What does His return mean to you?

Christ's return has double messages like a double-edged sword. To those who live a life in darkness, the message of Christ's return is a warning of judgment and a wake up call (1 Thessalonians 5:2–3, 6–7). Christ's parable of the five foolish bridegrooms and five wise bridegrooms explains the contrasting responses of the two groups very well (Matthew 25:1–13).

Christ's return is a message of hope for this century, especially to those who are waiting for Him to come back (1 Thessalonians 4:13– 18, 5:9–10; Matthew 25:1–13).

> "After that, we who are still alive and are left will be caught up together with them in the clouds to meet the Lord in the air. And so we will be with the Lord forever. Therefore encourage each other with these words" (1 Thessalonians 4:17–18).

> "For God did not appoint us to suffer wrath but to receive salvation through our Lord Jesus Christ. He died for us so that, whether we are awake or asleep, we may live together with him" (1 Thessalonians 5:9–10).

How Do We Get Ready for His Return?

How does the message of Christ's return impact your thought and make you feel?

Christ's return is similar to parents coming back home after being out for a while. For kids who messed up their rooms, the message that their parents are coming home is not so pleasant, yet for those who behaved and did their chores, it is an exciting and joyful message.

You should expect and believe that His return is imminent, just as the first century Christians did. It is not a threatening message; it is thrilling, because it gives us *hope*.

The Apostle John, who suffered loneliness and persecution on an isolated island, welcomed the Lord's imminent return. "Yes, I am coming soon," Jesus said. "Amen. Come, Lord Jesus," John responded (Revelation 22:20).

To each individual, Christ's coming back is a hopeful message because it brings us hope of eternity and God's peaceful kingdom.

To the world, the second coming is the hope of the generations because Jesus Christ, who is faithful and true, is coming as the righteous new leader of the world; He will end the chaos, suffering, disasters, and all the problems that have accumulated throughout human history.

In his book, *The Coming World Leader*, the Reverend David Hocking explains Christ's return as the hope of the generations because it will be the time when the new world leader arrives.

To those who are awaiting His return, His coming is a blessing and a hope as it would be a disastrous day for those who are against to Christ. All of us wonder about the future of our nation, our family and ourselves. What fortunes, good or evil, would form tomorrow, next week, next year? Do the leading economic factors foretell a coming collapse? Do the power summits hold out any hope for prevention of a Bio-Chemical and nuclear war? Is there going to be a natural catastrophe? Will I fall into car accident? Everything is uncertain in the future and it makes people anxious about tomorrow. Some people go to fortune-teller to cope with the problem of anxiety. Others just worry and wait for the inevitable events. Some people just hope that it would not happen in their lifetime. However, we, Christians can see through it and find the light that would be filled with the hope and certainty. That hope is the sureness of the returning of Jesus Christ to establish His righteous and peaceful kingdom. He is coming world leader; under His reign all that is wrong will be made right.[52]

How do we get ready for His return? Do we have to sell all our possessions and donate all to the church or quit our jobs and go out to the street? Not at all!

We can be ready for His coming by continuing to walk in the light. Romans 13:12 says, "The night is far spent, the day is at hand: let us therefore cast off the works of darkness, and let us put on the armor of light" Stay in the light of salvation and get ready to accept His return.

Preach the good news as Christ asked us to do!

Do good things for your neighbors like a good Samaritan.

---

[52] David Hocking, *The Coming of the World Leader*, (Portland, OR: Multnomah, 1998), 7–8.

Yearn for the hope of nations, the Messiah, with the same high expectations Simeon had! (Luke 2:34)

For Reflection and Discussion

1. What is your personal view of the end of life?
2. What do you think about human history? Is it the endless repetition of a pattern and an endless circle, or does history have a starting and ending point? In other words, is it circular or linear?
3. How can we be sure that Jesus will come back?
4. When will the day of Christ's return be? What signs of His return will we see? What does this tell us about the importance of accepting His return?
5. What does Christ's second coming mean to you? What are the double messages of Christ's return? Is it a hopeful message or a terrifying warning message?
6. How do we get ready for Christ's return?

Live a hopeful life with the expectation that Christ will come back to you and the world.

BIBLIOGRAPHY

Dark - Personal Holocaust - The Jewish Magazine, March 2010 Edition www.jewishmag.com/142mag/holocaust . . . /holocaust_experience. htm (accessed on August 30, 2011)

Ackerley, Sandra K. (ackerley@uoguelph.ca),Department of Zoology, University of Guelph, Guelph, Ontario, Canada N1G 2W1. (accessed on 18 August, 2011)

Bishop, Jim, *The Days of Martin Luther King, Jr.* New York: G.P. Putnam's Sons, 1971.

Chapman, Gary. *The Five Love Languages*, Chicago: Northfield Publishing, 1992.

Erickson, Millard J. *Christian Theology*, Grand Rapids: Baker Book House, 1983.

Frankl, Viktor E. *Man's Searching for Meaning*, Boston: Wilsted & Taylor Publishing Services, A Light in the 1959.

Ganong. *Review of Medical Physiology, 22nd Edition.* Specialized form of muscle that is peculiar to the vertebrate heart, (From Wikipedia, the free encyclopedia (accessed on August 18, 2011)

Gonzalez, *Justo L. The Story of Christianity: The Early Church to the Present Day*, Peabody : Prince Press, 2009.

Hebrew alphabet - Wikipedia, the free encyclopedia en.wikipedia.org/wiki/Hebrew_alphabet (accessed on September 11, 2011)

Henrietta, Buckmaster, *Paul, A Man Who Changed the World*, McGraw-Hill Book Company, 1965.

Hocking, David. *The Coming of the World Leader*, Portland: Multnomah, 1998.

Hugo, Victor. *Les Miserables*, Fire Side Rockefeller Center, New York: Modern Library Classics A new Translation By Julie Rose, 2009.

Lapide, Phinhas in Hans Kung. *"Jesus in Conflict," a dialogue between Phinhas Lapide and Hans Kung*, in Signposts for the Future, edited by Hans Kung , New York: Doubleday, 1978.

La Sor, William Sanford, Hubbard, David Allan and Bush, Frederic William. *Old Testament Survey, The Message, Form, and Background of the Old Testament*, Grand Rapids: William B. Eerdmans Publishing Company, 1982.

Meyer, Joyce. *Seven Things that Steal Your Joy*, New York: Warner Books, 2004.

Normandy Landing, en.wikipedia.org/wiki/Normandy_landings (accessed on 29 August, 2011).

Peale, Norman Vincent. *The Power of Positive Thinking*, New York: Ballantine Books, 1952.

Pentecost, J. Dwight. *Your Adversary The Devil*, Grand Rapids: Kregel Publication, 1969.

Swindoll, Charles R. *Hope Again*, USA: W. Publishing Group Thomas Nelson, 1996.

Tanchum 1.1 cf. John Lightfoot, *A Commentary on the New Testament from the Talmud and Hebraica*, Grand Rapids: Baker Book House, 1979, vol. 2.

"The Pathos Behind Da Vinci's-Last Supper", Articles on Revelation File News Service, 1977. http://www.ichc.org/scratchpad/a44.htm. (accessed on August 20, 2011)

Tournier, Paul. *The Seasons of Life*, translated by John Gilmour, London: SCM Press, 1972.

Tzu, Sun. *The Art of War*, (6th century BC) Ch. 3, From Wikiquote, http://en.wikiquote.org/wiki/Sun_Tzu (accessed on August 25, 2011)

University of Guelph Developmental Biology ONLINE! web site (retrieved 2010-05-04) http://www.uoguelph.ca/zoology/ devobio/210labs/ muscle1.html(From Wikipedia, the freeencyclopedia Jump to: navigation, search) (accessed on August18, 2011)

Welcome to **Dongmakgol** (웰컴 투 동막골) korean film 2005, www.koreanmovie.com/Welcome_to_Dongmakgol_km491/ (accessed on August 18, 2011)

Wiesel, Elie. *Night*, New York: Hill and Wang, 1972. (Originally published, France, by Les Editions de Minuit, La Nuit, 1958)

Zettersten, Rolf. *Dr. Dobson: Turning Hearts Toward the Home*, Dallas: W Publishing Group, 1992.

www.ingramcontent.com/pod-product-compliance
Lightning Source LLC
Chambersburg PA
CBHW020525080526
44583CB00013B/744